To my wife Audrey.
—Richard Featheringham

To Lisa and Ron.
—Bonni Perrott Baker

Applications in
Business Communication

Communicating at

Richard Featheringham
Central Michigan University

Bonni Penix Baker
Siena College

SOUTH-WESTERN
★
THOMSON LEARNING

Australia · Canada · Mexico · Singapore · Spain · United Kingdom · United States

Applications in Business Communication: Communicating at GEI
by Richard D. Featheringham and Bonni Perrott Baker.

Publisher: Dave Shaut
Acquisitions Editor: Pamela M. Person
Developmental Editor: Tina Edmondson and Jennifer Elworth
Marketing Manager: Rob Bloom
Production Editor: Amy S. Gabriel
Manufacturing Coordinator: Sandee Milewski
Cover and Internal Design: Jennifer Lambert, Jen2 Design, Cincinnati
Cover Image: © Wendy Grossman, Stock Illustration Source
Production House: Trejo Production
Printer: Quebecor World—Taunton, MA

Printed in the United States of America
1 2 3 4 5 03 02 01 00

For more information contact South-Western, 5101 Madison Road, Cincinnati, Ohio, 45227 or find us on the Internet at http://www.swcollege.com

For permission to use material from this text or product, contact us by
• **telephone: 1-800-730-2214**
• **fax: 1-800-730-2215**
• **web: http://www.thomsonrights.com**

Library of Congress Cataloging-in-Publication Data
Featheringham, Richard.
    Applications in business communication : communicating at GEI / Richard D. Featheringham, Bonni Perrott Baker.
        p. cm.
      ISBN 0-324-01405-8 (alk. paper)
      I. Business communication.   I. Baker, Bonni Perrott   II. Title.
    HF5718.F43 2000
    658.4'5—dc21
    00-058834

About the Authors

Dr. Richard D. Featheringham

Dr. Richard D. Featheringham has been teaching business communications for the Department of Business Information Systems at Central Michigan University since 1971. He also teaches courses in business report writing and business ethics.

He has given presentations on the national level and the international level and has researched and written extensively in the areas of national and international business communications, business ethics, business information systems, and methodology for teaching. Dr. Featheringham received the Excellence in Teaching award from Central Michigan University, the College of Business Administration (CMU) Dean's Outstanding Teaching Award, the College of Business Ameritech Excellence in Teaching Award, and the Outstanding Educator of the Year award from the National Court Reporters Association. He was recently nominated by the president of Central Michigan University for the U.S. Professors of the Year Program. Before coming to Central Michigan University, he received the Outstanding Faculty Member Award, Alumni Distinguished Teacher of the Year Award, and Outstanding Teacher in the College of Business Administration Award at Kent State University.

Dr. Featheringham has consulted in the field of business communications. As a former court reporter, Dr. Featheringham developed the Court Reporting Program at Central Michigan University.

Professor Bonni Perrott Baker

Professor Bonni Perrott Baker has taught at Siena College in Loudonville, New York, since 1987, in the Marketing and Management Department of the Business Division. She teaches courses in Business Communications, Human Resource Management, and Performance Appraisal, Work Behavior, and Motivation. While at Siena, Professor Baker has served on the Human Rights Committee, coordinated the International Certificate Program, the Study Abroad Program, and the Marketing and Management Internship Program. She has facilitated interactive student education programs nationally and internationally, traveling to Ukraine and Egypt. During a sabbatical, she taught International Management in Lyon, France. In 1999, Professor Baker was a nominee for the Siena College Teacher of the Year award, and received the "Excellence in Education" Award presented by the American Lung Association for her work with interns. In April 2000, she received the Academy of Business Administration's First Annual Sammy Amin Teaching Excellence Award, and she was nominated for "Who's Who Among Outstanding Educators" for the 2000–2001 publication of *The National Dean's List*.

Many companies in the Northeast and Midwest consult Professor Baker in the area of communications and human resource management. Her particular areas of expertise include interoffice communication, training and development of employees, and motivation.

Before joining Siena, Professor Baker was vice-president of Human Resource Management for two Columbus, Ohio, savings' associations. She also served in several key human resource positions in Philadelphia, Pennsylvania, and Pittsfield, Massachusetts.

Contents

Preface

Welcome to Goodtimes Enterprises, Inc. (GEI). *Applications in Business Communication* simulates a hypothetical company that specializes in producing indoor and outdoor leisure-time products, giving students the opportunity to apply business communication skills in a real-life setting. Students work in self-managed work teams to solve real-life problems facing businesses today. The instructor acts as CEO of GEI.

This product was developed because the authors believe that when students are able to actively take part in learning the subject matter and relate it to their daily lives, they develop the higher-order skills of analysis, synthesis, and evaluation. Additionally, working collaboratively toward a single goal provides students with an understanding of the importance of teamwork. Such an understanding equips students with necessary tools to meet the challenges of today's workplace. The activities are offered to enhance understanding about group dynamics, and to stimulate critical thinking.

Some of the activities at GEI in which you may become involved are designed to promote business-connected learning. Here are just a few of them:

- The classroom is designed as a business enterprise.
- All assignments given and received by the CEO include a memo of transmittal.
- Employees (students) prepare and use company stationery, business cards, team charter, and other items that promote the business-connected learning.
- All reports include an executive summary.
- Each team is responsible for preparing an in-house publication.
- Frequent in-house seminars and workshops are held. Guest speakers talk to teams on a variety of subjects (for example, how to give an effective business presentation or conduct a business meeting, effective use of graphics, multiculturalism, conducting business internationally, and so forth.)
- Debates are held on current issues in business.
- Field trips to business installations may be scheduled.
- Employees have a chance to appear on television (VCR recording) to justify a position and/or take a position on a matter of importance to the company.
- Role playing is an integral part of the course.
- The CEO evaluates student work in light of company objectives.
- Other materials teams may be asked to use or to prepare are evaluation forms, case problems, and team projects.

The GEI applications are designed to help students prepare for responsible participation in an increasingly diverse world. This experience will help them improve their relationship skills for future management roles by:

1. Creating a better understanding of their own beliefs about workplace behavior.
2. Providing examples of how choices are made between alternative courses of action in the workplace.

3. Preparing for future learning.

4. Developing an understanding of how teamwork and the group process can be used in project completion.

5. Reducing the differences between the theoretical world of the classroom and the realities of the business world.

Good luck with your employment at GEI.

Acknowledgments

Bonni Perrott Baker would like to extend her appreciation to Richard Featheringham, who invited her to join him in this endeavor, and thank him for his encouragement and helpful suggestions throughout the project.

Many people have assisted in making this book possible. She is especially grateful to her students, who keep her active and motivated in the classroom. Their feedback and reactions to the applications in this book aided in creating a better product.

She extends a special thanks to Dr. Timoth Lederman and Dr. James Nolan of Siena College who permitted the flexibility in her teaching schedule to allow the time needed for writing. She is also grateful to colleagues Fred Decasperis, Chuck Seifert, Terry Curran, Fareed Munir, Chitra Rajan, Susan Switzer, and Larry Thomas for their advice and input; to Brother John Mahon for his perspective and prayers; and to Lisa and Ron Perrott for their continuing support and love.

Richard Featheringham extends his thanks and appreciation to all those students, who over the years have challenged and motivated him to do a better job in the classroom. A special thank you goes to his children and their spouses, Wendy and Steve and children, Alyssa, Tyler, and Jacob; Amy and Scott and children, Lucas and Holly; Julie and James and their daughter, Lauren; and to his son, Rick.

A special thank you goes to his wife Audrey for her encouragement in his pursuit and development of this project and for her continuing support and love.

Special thanks goes to the coauthor Bonni Perrott Baker for a wealth of ideas, constant encouragement, and a willingness to tackle a huge undertaking.

The authors realize this book would have been impossible without the patient and outstanding work of the staff at South-Western. They are especially indebted to Pamela Person, Tina Edmondson, Jennifer Elworth, and Amy S. Gabriel, who helped with the manuscript and kept them on track.

The authors also wish to acknowledge their grateful appreciation for the careful reviews and suggestions made by the following professors:

Martha Kuchar
Roanoke College

Loise Rehling
San Francisco University

Janel Bloch
Iowa State University

Jack Bedell
Southeastern Louisiana University

Roberta Krapels
University of Mississippi

Bernadette Longo
Clemson University

Glynna Morse
Georgia College & State University

Jim Rucker
Fort Hays State University

Beryl McEwen
North Carolina A&T State University

Shawn Carraher
Indiana University Northwest

Richard Hogrefe
Riverside Community College

Ann Beebe
Lansing Community College

Ruthann Dirks
Emporia State University

Roosevelt Butler
The College of New Jersey

Jeffrey Phillips
Northwood University

Introduction

About the Company

The company, Goodtimes Enterprises, Inc. (GEI), for which you will be working this semester, produces indoor and outdoor leisure-time products. It operates three plants, one in Mt. Pleasant, Michigan, another in Albany, New York, and the third in Albuquerque, New Mexico. It does a nationwide business and is growing annually. GEI has built its reputation by offering quality products, excellent customer service, and fair prices. Indoor products include bowling equipment and basketballs. The outdoor division produces products such as golf gadgets and equipment; baseball, football, and hockey equipment; and play gyms for children.

GEI employs 450 people, 275 of them in their Mt. Pleasant plant, 100 in the Albuquerque plant, and 75 in the Albany plant. The company believes in using self-managed work teams, which operate under fairly strict company guidelines. To date, this approach has worked successfully, and productivity standards are high. Employees and managers know their individual responsibilities, yet work well together.

Recently, competitors of GEI have expanded globally, so the company's Research and Development Department is currently conducting market research to determine if it will benefit their bottom line to open subsidiaries in foreign countries. The company knows it will face difficulties if it decides to expand its product line to the world market. It realizes that if it is to be successful internationally it will have to prepare its employees to be culturally flexible enough to meet the global challenge.

Company History

GEI was founded in 1987 by Larry Switzer, its current president and chief executive officer. He recognized that people are more and more concerned about their quality of life, especially in their leisure-time activities. After extensive market research indicated that this is a growth market, he decided to start GEI.

Because Larry's expertise was primarily in manufacturing and production, he realized he would need assistance in other areas of the business. He offered Lourdes Morales, a marketing executive, the opportunity to join GEI in its development phase. She accepted this challenge and joined the company at its inception.

Startup funds came from a personal investment of $75,000 each from Larry and Lourdes, and a $100,000 loan from the U.S. Small Business Administration. GEI did not begin production in its first year of operations. Its business activities consisted principally of marketing research, product development and testing, and raising additional capital to sustain its business activities.

As the business grew, Larry and Lourdes realized that they needed someone with expertise in financial management and in human resources, particularly in staffing and training. Thus, they added two people to the senior staff: Susan

Thomas as vice president of human resources, and Fareed Rajan as financial vice president. As is often the case in small companies, the four executive officers are centralized and are located in the Mt. Pleasant plant. By its third year in operations, GEI had become profitable, mainly because of careful financial management and the success of two products, the *Mr. Mister* and the *Wolverine Off-Road Machine*.

Employee Profiles

President and CEO—Mr. Larry Switzer

Larry Switzer, founder of GEI, has an MBA from the University of Chicago. Because he likes to keep abreast of day-to-day operations, he uses a management-by-walking-around approach in the business. His management philosophy encourages open communication that helps keep employees motivated. Larry believes in delegation of authority and welcomes and expects ideas on how to improve and/or create products and working conditions from all employees. He also expects 100 percent commitment from his employees. His office is located in the Mt. Pleasant plant, but since the company has expanded, he travels to each of the other plants at least once a month. Larry approves all major manufacturing and production decisions.

Executive Vice President, Marketing and Sales— Ms. Lourdes Morales

Lourdes Morales had worked for a moderately successful family-run marketing firm for seven years as the head of marketing research. She felt the company was carrying too many family members and that there was little chance of promotion. She holds a master's degree in international marketing and has wanted to make an upward move in her career for the past two years. When Larry approached her about investing in and working with him in GEI, she felt it was a perfect match. The marketing plan she has developed includes major product and sales promotion ideas, and targeting new markets both nationally and internationally. Lourdes is well respected throughout the company.

Vice President, Finance—Mr. Fareed Rajan

Fareed Rajan is eager to keep GEI financially strong and is committed to helping it develop to its full potential. He has an MBA and holds the professional designation certified financial advisor (CFA). Fareed has worked for 10 years in the leisure and sports products field and welcomes the challenge of his new position. He is intent on cost control and efficiency and has asked each project management team to develop and submit a budget to him, which he intends to review to see where costs can be reduced. He is viewed as hard driving and tough but fair by most of the project managers, and he has a good working relationship with Larry, Lourdes, and Susan.

Vice President, Human Resources—Ms. Susan Thomas

Susan Thomas holds a master's degree in organizational behavior. Her previous position, which she held for six years, was human resource director for a company that made plastic parts for children's toys. Her specialty is the training and development of employees. Susan takes pride in hiring the right person for each position, and was instrumental in developing the self-managed project teams that GEI uses throughout the company. She is very competent and has a flair for thinking creatively. She shares the other executives' vision for the company, and is well liked by everyone throughout the organization, particularly the project managers. One of her goals is to help the company remain nonunion through quality of work life programs and by providing excellent benefits.

Instructions to Employees

Now in its 12th year, GEI has determined that to stay competitive in the marketplace, it needs to develop some new and innovative products that are compatible with existing leisure-time products. During the course of this semester, your instructor will act as the CEO of GEI, and you will become virtual employees of GEI.

Your CEO/instructor will usually begin each class with a briefing and planning session about the applications that you will be working on during that class session. He or she will assign you to a self-managed project team, which will be creating these new products for GEI. Appliction 1 of the text discusses "Teamwork in Business," which gives each team the necessary information about roles, group norms, and reporting structures. Your CEO may want to assign that as your first application when he or she selects the teams.

Your CEO will determine which applications are to be done individually and which will be team-based projects. Individual team members are always accountable for their own work, and it is possible to get "fired" from a team if you do not do your assigned tasks. The CEO will explain your responsibilities during the briefing sessions. Many of your assignments will come to you in the form of a memo from one of the four executive officers of GEI.

The CEO/instructor will decide the size of each team. Once each team is established and a project manager has been chosen, the team will be given raw materials with which to create a new leisure-time product for GEI. Usually the materials distributed to you will be Tinkertoys, Legos, or Lincoln Logs, but each CEO will decide that, and will tell you how long you will have to complete this first part of the assignment.

Each section of this applications book presents a number of active learning communication exercises and projects for use in class and for homework. The sections contain information about basic and international business communication concepts and practices. At the end of each application you will find a list of job responsibilities that you must complete. Some of these may relate to *teamwork*, *ethics*, *technology*, or *diversity* issues. Every application may not include all of these topics, but there will be a logo for each one so that you can easily recognize the topic covered in the activity. The logos will look like this:

Once your team's product has been developed and completed, team members should name the product and decide its function. Remember, your team is a project management team that is part of GEI's indoor or outdoor division, depending on the kind of product the team has created. Have fun! Welcome to Goodtimes Enterprises, Inc.

Teamwork in Business

GEI's executive staff know the value of "empowering" their employees. They view empowerment as a valuable management technique because it transfers much of the decision-making and problem-solving responsibilities from upper-level management to employees who are in the best position to make those decisions. GEI believes empowered employees feel more committed to the organization and its goals and are more enthusiastic about their work.

That is why Susan Thomas introduced self-managed project teams to GEI when she joined the company. She believes that self-managed teams empower employees because they make decisions by consensus, accept individual and mutual responsibility, and know what each team member's duties are so they can work together to achieve common goals. The CEO read about the positive effects that self-managed teams can have in the workplace and has enthusiastically endorsed the work team concept.

Susan knows the most effective teams achieve a high level of productivity while maintaining close interpersonal relationship among members, but that conflict can occur occasionally. To help GEI's self-managed teams work at their optimum she periodically gets feedback from the project managers about each teams' performance. One of the project managers expressed concern at the meeting about some problems that were occurring in her team.

"I've had a problem with some absenteeism among team members and the tardiness of other team members to some of our scheduled meetings."

Another project manager chimed in, "Yes, I know what you mean. I've had difficulty setting up meeting times . . . someone always complains it's not at a convenient time. When I do hold meetings, it seems as if very little gets accomplished, and there is often unequal participation of team members."

A third manager offered, "We seem to have some personality conflicts on our team, and some members complain they do not have time to complete the assignments that are given to them."

Susan realized some time had to be set aside for reviewing how the teams were operating and what could be done to keep them functioning as integrated and empowered teams. After this meeting, she sent you and the other Project Directors this memo requesting the following information.

GEI

12345 GEI Place   Mt. Pleasant, Michigan 48859   517.555.1000

TO: Project Directors

FROM: Susan Thomas, VP Human Resources

DATE: January 5, 200-

SUBJECT: Summary Role Descriptions

So that each team member may work most efficiently toward the common goals of GEI, it is important that he or she identifies his or her role and responsibilities. This will facilitate the accomplishment of tasks in the most efficient manner.

A summary role description needs to be developed for each team member that will briefly explain what the team member actually does. It should also include a job title. Some questions to ask when writing the role summary are:

1. What is the job title?

2. What are the major duties of the position?

3. Are there any special activities in which the team member participates?

Before you begin writing the individual role summaries, I suggest that you hold a team meeting to consider how you wish to operate as a team and what responsibilities each team member will have. You may want to ask team members to interview each other to develop a list of role duties. To aid you in this process, I have attached a sample role summary of my position and that of the CEO.

Job Responsibilities

teamwork

1. Talk to other team members to reach consensus about each member's duties and then write a role summary of the responsibilities you have within your team. Your boss may give you additional guidelines on writing a role summary.

2. Discuss some potential or real problems that can or have occurred within your team. What can you do to prevent them in the future? List several problems your team has or might encounter and how the team has handled and solved them. As a team, prepare a five-minute presentation for the rest of the class that deals with the causes of and possible solutions to these problems. Include a plan for how the team will handle conflict when it occurs. Your boss will tell you how long you have to prepare the presentation.

3. One member of your team missed an important meeting this morning. He was supposed to present some information that the team needed to have before it could proceed further on a particular project. This is not the first time this has happened. But, this time, there is a good chance the team will miss the deadline set for the project. You know he overslept because he had been out partying the previous night, but when he does arrive, he says he was held up in traffic because of an accident. What do you do? Consider the ethical issues associated with your decision, including the possible effect on your relationship with him and other members of your team.

Sample Summary Role Descriptions

Chief Executive Officer

The chief executive officer of GEI is directly responsible for implementing and executing the general policies of GEI and for providing leadership and general direction to the employees of GEI, and is accountable for the successful operation of the company's business.

Vice President of Human Resources

The vice president of human resources is responsible for developing and implementing GEI's human resource policies and the hiring, training, and development of employees. The incumbent is also responsible for maintaining an open line of communication between the project teams and senior management.

Using Technology in Business Communication

Technology is a pervasive part of any business today, and GEI takes advantage of technology in their daily operations. At a recent senior staff meeting, Larry Switzer asked his staff what forms of technology they expected the project teams to use when they communicated with them.

"When I ask for an oral presentation, I expect PowerPoint to be used to enhance the presentation," Lourdes Morales said, "and I expect them to be able to do Internet searches to review our competitor's Web pages when we need to learn information about them."

Larry agreed. "Yes, they must be able to do that. Do all employees know how to use the PowerPoint presentation software we've just purchased? I, too, expect them to use it when giving presentations to upper management. PowerPoint gives them everything they need to create a high-quality presentation using text, outlining, drawing, graphing, clip art, and so on."

"I can take care of ensuring employees are trained in PowerPoint," said Fareed Rajan. "I do also think that the Internet is a very powerful tool for GEI. I have often heard the marketers say it is indispensable when researching our competition. It can also be an invaluable source of information for researching reports and other materials. I think we should also make sure GEI employees are trained in how to use the Internet to help them complete their job responsibilities."

"Very good point!" Larry smiled. "Our employees also use e-mail and electronic conferencing when communicating with each other, especially when the employees are located at different plants. We must do an inventory of our present hardware and software to be sure it meets our employees' technological needs."

"Sure, boss," Fareed replied.

"Larry, you know what might be a good way to get employees up to speed with technology is to have a contest among the project teams to see who can design the best project team letterhead," said Susan Thomas. "They can design this letterhead on a word processor or graphics program, and then use this letterhead to submit materials as they work on their various projects. They could also design their own business cards, which would help represent the company in the best possible light."

"That's a great idea, Susan!" said Larry. "Can you please arrange that?"

As you can see, GEI expects its employees to embrace technology and to use it to be more efficient, productive, and professional. E-mail is a technology that makes it easy to correspond quickly with everyone within GEI. As you work for GEI, you may very well send assignments to your CEO or other team members by e-mail. You also know that you will be expected to prepare team and individual oral presentations that will be enhanced with presentation software. These are only a few of the types of technology you will deal with as you work on various projects for GEI. Which technology tools you decide to use depend on your audience, the type of message you are sending, and what technologies are available to you.

After the staff meeting, you find the following two memos in your mailbox from Larry and Susan.

12345 GEI Place　　　　**Mt. Pleasant, Michigan 48859**　　　　**517.555.1000**

TO:　　　　Project Directors

FROM:　　　Larry Switzer, CEO, and Susan Thomas, VP Human Resources

DATE:　　　September 2, 200-

SUBJECT:　Designing a New Letterhead

GEI is sponsoring a contest between all work teams to design a letterhead for their team. Each team will submit their entry to Larry for judging. All entries will be reviewed by the senior management team, who will decide the winning entry. The winning team will be given a pizza party at Joe's Pizza.

Keep in mind that the your team letterhead will represent GEI. It should be professional, businesslike, and in good taste. Remember, too, that letterheads usually take up 2 to 2½ inches at the top of the paper. If possible, the letterhead should be designed on the computer using a word processor or graphics program.

In the future, the project teams will use the letterhead they have designed to submit all project materials to GEI.

The contest deadline is _____. Good luck! Have fun!

12345 GEI Place   **Mt. Pleasant, Michigan 48859**   **517.555.1000**

TO: Project Directors

FROM: Lourdes Morales, VP Marketing and Sales

DATE: September 4, 200-

SUBJECT: Preparing Your Business Card

Every team member should have a business card. Please design one for yourself. Include your name and all essential company information needed by customers and others to contact you. You may wish to use a picture or a short logo on your card.

If someone on your project team has business card software on his/her computer, assign that person the responsibility of preparing several copies of the cards for each team member. If no one has the software, the word processing software in the Information and Technology Services Department has the capability to produce excellent business cards.

Please turn in business cards to me by_____.

Job Responsibilities

1. Come up with a list of at least 15 items that make presentation software an asset in a professional presentation. To research your points, use the Internet, view the software, and read computer books/manuals or a textbook. Are there any cons to using technology in a presentation? Discuss your thoughts in class with the rest of GEI's employees. Use the blackboard or an overhead projector to compile a complete list of everyone's comments, and discuss.

2. Search the Internet for the Web pages of two or three corporations that compete with GEI in the leisure goods market. You might begin by looking at some common search engines such as **www.search.com, www.yahoo.com, www.altavista.com,** or **www.excite.com.** Compare and contrast the Web sites. What do they do well? Which one is the most appealing and why? Was one more easy to navigate and what made it that way? Can you think of any ways

these companies might enhance their site? Write a short memo to Fareed concerning this competitive activity and what GEI should do if a company Web site is launched. Submit printouts of the Web pages if at all possible.

3. Prepare your business card. Before you create your own, review at least four cards from people who have them. What stands out on the cards you reviewed as a positive? What do you dislike about the cards? Is all the information you would need on the card? Ask for helpful feedback from other team members about your card. Did you use clip art or other graphic capabilities?

4. Design a team letterhead to enter into the contest. Brainstorm with other team members to get some creative ideas, and study letterheads from other companies before you begin your design. Include the team name, address, telephone, fax, and any other material and information the team feels is appropriate. Does it need some kind of logo or simple design?

5. GEI has a company policy that prohibits personal use of computers. You have a PC on your desk that gives you access to e-mail and Internet resources, and occasionally you use them for personal mail and searches when not under time pressure for work assignments. Is this a big deal or not? Discuss the ethical implications of doing this with the rest of the class. Note that some companies have a zero tolerance policy for employees who violate computer policies. Are such policies too strict?

Developing a Code of Ethics

Susan Thomas has been serving as head of a company committee on ethics. She was overheard the other day saying to Larry Switzer that the Code of Ethics at GEI needs some revisions.

"Ethical treatment of employees, customers, stockholders, and employers is critical to the success of the business," Susan said to Larry. "Our ethical code of conduct could be revamped in several areas. I can share with you the results of the research we have done if you like."

Larry has viewed the research and agrees with Susan. Therefore, the following memo appeared in your mailbox today.

| 12345 GEI Place | Mt. Pleasant, Michigan 48859 | 517.555.1000 |

TO:	Project Directors
FROM:	Larry Switzer, CEO
DATE:	February 1, 200-
SUBJECT:	Preparing a Code of Ethics

After an ethical audit by the ad hoc committee on ethics, GEI was found to be in violation of its ethical codes. The codes are antiquated and outdated. Please prepare a preliminary code of ethics for the company. The ethics audit committee surveyed customers, clients, the public, our employees, and the top executives for their evaluation of our ethical practices. The results of that audit single out the following areas that need to be revised and included in the code:

- Quality and safety of products and services
- Equal opportunity employment
- Compliance with laws and regulations
- Safety in the workplace and environment

Additional areas you may wish to specifically include are sexual harassment, giving of gifts, and conflicting roles.

Please carefully study the former code of ethics (attached). Also, you may wish to look at other codes of ethics on the Internet or in the library. Study as many codes of ethics that you can come up with so that you will have many ideas of what other companies' codes of ethics look like.

Since there is no one single format for codes of ethics, you should come up with a code that is easy to read and to understand. The format should be such that people want to read through it. Codes of ethics usually have three divisions:

- An introductory statement
- The code itself
- A concluding statement

Job Responsibilities

teamwork

1. Read both of the provided codes of ethics for GEI. Example 3.1 is the code for 1999; Example 3.2 is the revised code for this year. Discuss the various ways in which the code was revised from 1999 to the current code. Begin to plan the revision you will write of the code by making a list of items that should be addressed. Are there any current events in the news that might have impact on the new code of ethics?

diversity

2. What diversity issues might you need to consider when you revise the code? How are the employees affected? Is the code fair to all employees and to everyone in the company? Discuss with your teammates. Present your oral discussion results to the remainder of the company and solicit suggestions from them concerning diversity.

technology

3. Use the Internet to search for codes of ethics that guide other companies. Share the details of at least three codes with your classmates as a way to help you write the ethical code for GEI. Point out the differences and the similarities in the codes. Take part in an entire company discussion on the different codes.

4. Consider all the research and discussion you have performed and draft a new code of ethics. Present the preliminary GEI code of ethics orally to the rest of the company. Be prepared to answer any questions that arise.

5. After you have presented the code of ethics to the company, incorporate whatever suggestions you heard that would strengthen the final code of ethics for GEI. Prepare a final written copy of the GEI code of ethics for the current year.

Example 3.1   Company code of ethics.

Goodtimes Enterprises, Inc., Code of Ethics

January 1, 1999

GEI's goal is to treat each customer with respect and make every effort to promote customer satisfaction and conduct business honestly, fairly, and with integrity. We also provide a diverse and safe workplace where everyone receives equal opportunity.

The privilege of membership in this company carries with it the responsibility of maintaining and furthering the objectives of the company. Toward this end, the following standards are required:

1. An employee must agree to share the responsibility of furthering mutual trust and respect between the company and the public by conducting his or her business with honesty, fairness, and integrity. Employees will exercise common sense and courtesy in dealing with each other and the public.

2. An employee is responsible for the accurate description of all items offered for sale. All significant information must be disclosed to the customers. A full cash refund will be given to the buyer if there is any misrepresentation of the product sold.

3. An employee shall resolve any claims or disputes over the product by abiding by the decision of the Board of Directors relating to any complaint or dispute. Any violation of the employee by-laws, guidelines, code, or policies may be grounds for fine, censure, suspension, or expulsion from the company.

4. An employee must recognize that he or she is obligated to conduct business in accordance with all applicable laws, guidelines, and codes.

5. An employee shall cooperate with the company and legal authorities in any effort to recover or return stolen products and apprehend and prosecute those responsible for the theft. Furthermore, an employee will cooperate with the company on any inquiries on thefts, suspicious transactions, bad credit risks, offers of doubtful product or materials, and related matters.

6. The company shall produce and guarantee the quality and safety of the company's products and services.

7. The company shall offer equal opportunity employment and try to promote from within the company before going outside the company.

8. The company shall remain in compliance with all relevant laws and regulations, including environmental concerns.

9. The company shall provide a safe workplace and environment for its employees and customers.

10. An employee must respect other employees and customers by abiding by sexual harassment policies.

11. An employee must never offer a bribe or gift to current or potential customers or clients to ensure a purchase, sale, or investment.

GEI's code of ethics provides a clear understanding of the company's policies. Top management encourages ethical awareness in the company through their care and support of ethical training, sexual harassment awareness, and other similar programs. Our goal is to maintain our strong ethical climate. We also strive to provide an appealing work environment to increase employee loyalty, motivation, and morale. Our biggest goal, however, is to enhance the public's image of our company. We encourage honesty, loyalty, fairness, responsibility, accountability, and due care among all employees, including executive-level employees who set the examples for the rest of the company.

Example 3.2   Revised company code of ethics.

Goodtimes Enterprises, Inc. Code of Ethics

Revised January 1, 200-

In order to uphold the positive image of GEI, we value and enforce the following qualities of our employees, stakeholders, customers, suppliers, and customers:

- Honesty, truthfulness, and sincerity
- Integrity of the highest order
- Trustworthiness and the ability to fulfill commitments
- Fairness and equal treatment of all individuals
- Respect for others by being courteous and considerate
- Diligence by being reliable and seeking the pursuit of excellence

1. We will manufacture products and provide services consistent with and surpassing quality and safety standards.

2. We guarantee customer satisfaction with each of our products and services.

3. We will continually review and adapt to changing consumer needs and trends in the marketplace.

4. We actively support and uphold the importance of family and the personal needs of all employees.

5. We will offer variety in the scheduling needs of our employees without detracting from the excellence of other employees and our organization as a whole.

6. As an equal opportunity employer, we support and encourage diversity in the workplace. All programs, practices, and operations prohibit discrimination because of race, color, religion, gender, national origin, political affiliation, physical handicap, age, marital status, or sexual orientation.

7. The company and its officials, employees, and representatives will obey all laws and regulations.

8. We will adapt to any changes in regulations and laws related to our organization's operations.

9. We pledge to protect our employees and our community by going above and beyond the requirements of the Occupational Safety and Health Act (OSHA).

10. We will strictly enforce and penalize all violations of copyright laws concerning software and other company materials.

GEI's code of ethics is designed to create a pleasant working place in order to maintain a strong ethical climate. In addition, we strive to enhance the public image of GEI.

APPLICATION 4

Communicating Across Cultures

As you learned when you joined GEI, the company is expanding their market globally. Because of this, there is increased awareness and concern at all levels about how to best communicate with peoples from other cultures. Your CEO realizes that being an effective communicator in a cross-cultural situation can be challenging. Therefore, the following memo has been drafted and sent to all employees and project teams for their information.

GEI

12345 GEI Place   **Mt. Pleasant, Michigan 48859**   **517.555.1000**

TO: All Employees

FROM: Larry Switzer, CEO

DATE: February 15, 200-

SUBJECT: Writing a Letter to an International Company

When writing to someone in another country, find out all you can about how the people in the country "context." That is, how do they communicate? Are they very brisk and want to get right to the point, or are they more laid back and send a lot of nonverbal cues?

Two types of contexting exist: those people who live in high-context countries, and those who live in low-context countries.

High-Context Countries

In high-context countries, people do not feel comfortable committing themselves initially. Therefore, people in these countries may seem intentionally vague. Examples of high context countries are Japan, China, and many of the Asian countries. Most high-context cultures rely on personal relationships to best establish the trust and background information necessary for continuing communications. **Persons from high-context countries will seem to rely on *how* you express your message rather than on *what* you actually said.**

When you are writing or speaking to people in high-context countries, use the *inductive (indirect)* approach to communication. The steps are as follows:

- Begin with a pleasant opening. Talking about the weather or about the family is considered polite in high-context countries.

- Give an explanation or reasons you are writing. Then state the major objective of your letter (e.g., to schedule a meeting, to have a room reserved, or something similar).

- Close with a pleasant thought. Be as polite as possible, often incorporating personal relationship information while doing so.

Attached to this memo is a copy of a letter from a Japanese educator to a friend in America. Notice how he follows the inductive approach (see Example 4.1).

Low-Context Countries

A person from a low-context culture may seem blunt or even rude in stating his or her position. Such communications are not considered rude in that culture.

Low-context people rely heavily on rules and regulations. Germany, Holland, and many other northern European countries are low-context cultures. Sometimes you may even think that when communicating with these people, they will state what you think to be obvious. Low-context cultures generally separate business communication from the personal relationships of the communicators. Business is business; personal communication is personal communication. **Persons in low-context countries are interested in explicit verbal communication to interpret what is meant. They are interested in *what* you actually say.**

A good plan for communicating with low-context people, either orally or in writing, is the use of the *deductive (or direct)* plan for communication:

- State the objective of the communication up front.
- Give reasons to support the objective.
- Use a pleasant closing. Do not include any personal information, however.

See the letter (Example 4.2) from an American sales manager to a customer in Germany.

General Suggestions

Here are some suggestions to use when writing or speaking with someone in another country:

- Find out if the person is from a low-context or high-context country. Use the Internet and the library for your research.

- Use expressions that are easily understood by international people. Do not use a lot of American idioms (speech that means something to us but should not be taken literally by others; e.g., "what's up?"—a person from another country may look up in the air if you use that expression. Many such expressions exist.). You can find lists of such idioms on the Internet and in the library.

- Do not talk or write about controversial items. When writing to a person from Japan, avoid talking about Pearl Harbor or Hiroshima. When writing to people in Germany, avoid talking or writing about the Nazi regime.

- Use short, simple sentences. Use short, simple paragraphs.

- Use graphics and visuals to get ideas across.

- Use a traditional format. You are not expected to know the letter styles of every country you write to. Use the standard American style. Your recipients will be happy to see what the American format is.

- If you can include a few words in the language of the recipient, such as thank you, good morning, or others, please do so. Recipients will be flattered that you took the time to say something in their language.

Job Responsibilities

1. Write a letter to a person in a Japan telling the person about one of the products that is available from GEI. Use the high-context style of writing. Assume any facts about the product you feel necessary.

2. Write the same letter to a person in a German company, using the low-context style of writing.

3. In teams, share your letters with each other. Compare and contrast the different ways you wrote the letter (inductive vs. deductive approach, closing, etc.) depending on the audience receiving your letters.

4. Use the Internet to find a list of American idioms. Are there any on the list that you don't even recognize? Type a list of idioms for your future reference.

5. Use the Internet to search for typical business hours in 10 or 15 countries. For instance, in the United States, work hours typically range from 8 to 4 or 9 to 5. Type a list of business hours that you can share with other members of the company so that you will have a listing of many countries and their typical business hours.

Example 4.1   Sample letter from a Japanese citizen.

September 17, 200-
Toyohashi, Aichi Prefecture

Jonathan R. Rosselli, Ph.D.
Professor, Department of Marketing
College of Business Administration
Central Michigan University
Mt. Pleasant, MI 48859

My dear Dr. Rosselli,

Hello, how are you? How about your weather now. The weather here is getting calm in September but at the end of August there were heavy rains somewhere in the northeast provinces, the vicinity where I live. Now in September, we can enjoy a very nice comfortable sky.

My company is sending me to Mt. Pleasant for a meeting with your company. I will leave Japan on December 2 and be in Mt. Pleasant on December 4. I will stay in the area until December 17.

I deeply request that you reserve a room for me at a local hotel. I am sorry to put you to so much trouble. I will need a room that will allow me to use my computer and fax machine. If you can do this for me, I will be very grateful.

I really wish you and Mrs. Rosselli could come for a visit with us in Toyohashi. We will be very happy to meet and welcome you any time. I do not believe that any earthquake could come up during the time you will be here.

With a hearty thanks to you again. Best wishes to all my friends in Michigan.

Sincerely yours,

Motohiko Oba
Chairman, Toyohashi Tatsuzawa Gakkan

Example 4.2   Sample letter to a person in a low-context country.

12345 GEI Place   **Mt. Pleasant, Michigan 48859**   **517.555.1000**

November 15, 200-

Herr Karl Weigland, Manager
Gifts from the Forest
Friedrichstrasse 47
70174 Frankfurt
GERMANY

Very Honorable Herr Weigland:

As the tourist season begins soon, we are happy to offer our new line of American sports clocks
to you to include in your stock. Last year, you bought three dozen of our clocks. We are very
grateful for your purchase. Because we have a good business relationship, we are now offering
you the opportunity to select what you want before we offer this line to other businesspeople.

Our sports clockmakers use only the finest materials. They are the best wood so that every hand
carved detail is beautiful and functional. All of our clocks are tested before they are painted, cali-
brated, and shipped. We provide a guarantee of five years on every clock you purchase from us.

Here is a copy of our newest brochure that describes and illustrates all of the models available.
As an expression of our appreciation for your past business, we will pay all of the shipping costs
for every clock you order before February 1.

Continued success in your business in Frankfurt.

With warm wishes,

Project Director

Listening Skills

At the weekly senior staff meeting, Larry Switzer told the group about a complaint he had received the previous week. The long-time customer had special ordered 7 gross of *Mr. Misters*, one of GEI most profitable products. The customer had requested extralarge sprinkler heads, but when they arrived they were the usual standard size. This was not the first time this customer's order had not been filled as requested. The customer was extremely irate and had threatened to end his business relationship with GEI.

"This whole incident could have been avoided if the project manager had listened more carefully." Larry sighed. "Not listening carefully to customers alienates them and loses profits for us! A tuned-in communicator and employee helps secure repeat business."

Susan Thomas nodded in agreement. "Not only that, boss, but when an effective project manager listens to team members and other employees, it increases morale and improves team interaction, which, in turn, presents a positive image to customers."

Lourdes Morales chimed in, "All our products must satisfy customer demand for quality and value. One of the most beneficial skills our employees can possess is that of being a good listener. We have to know what our customers want in order to achieve our sales goals."

"The problem is that hearing is automatic, but listening is not! Listening is an active skill that requires practice, but too many people just smile and say uh-huh while they are tuning out the person," Larry said. "Or they're distracted by something or worried about a report that needs to be finished, and the last thing on their minds is the customer who deserves their undivided attention. We've got to teach our employees to concentrate and stay focused when they are listening to a customer or another employee."

"I agree," said Lourdes. "I'll take care of sending out a memo regarding this important topic."

As a result of the meeting, this memo appears in your mailbox the following day.

12345 GEI Place   **Mt. Pleasant, Michigan 48859**   **517.555.1000**

TO:	All Employees
FROM:	Lourdes Morales, VP Marketing and Sales
DATE:	February 28, 200-
SUBJECT:	Improving Listening Skills

Sometimes we forget that communication is two way: giving and receiving. Many of us master the giving side: how to speak and write. But often we do not pay careful attention to the receiving side: listening.

Active Listening. If someone tells you what is desired but you do not listen well enough to fully understand what is expected, the communication has not been successful. When you don't listen carefully to a customer, to a fellow employee, or to a boss, it can mean lost sales, conflict with peers, and even a lost promotion. A good communicator must be not only a "good" listener, but an "active" listener as well. Remember, hearing is passive. Anyone can hear. Listening is active. It requires effort on the part of the receiver.

What is *active listening*? It is a conscious decision to take part in the communication process, by listening with more than your ears. You use your brain and knowledge as appropriate as you listen. Active listening maximizes your ability to better understand the needs of your customers and coworkers. Active listening allows you to give better, more appropriate feedback and advice, if and when it is needed. A sympathetic ear has great value in teamwork situations and in the workplace in general.

A tuned-in communicator tries to use active listening skills that show interest, understanding, and that elicit more information from the speaker by using:

1. **Use of verbal signals that signify your interest and attention**. Don't simply say "uh-huh" or "really." Use words that show you are truly listening such as:
   - Tell me more.
   - What do you mean by that?
   - What happened then?
   - What did you do as a result?

2. **Encouraging nonverbal signals**. These are supportive, interested facial expressions, nods of the head in understanding, and good eye contact. Some nonverbals can quickly become passive listening traits, however, so be on guard and concentrate on being an active listener.

3. **Restate or paraphrase what has been said.** Paraphrasing is a method of communication where the listener repeats the idea or content of what is being said. Not only

does this help the listener listen more carefully, it can also discourage misunderstandings in communication. When you paraphrase, you might begin with a phrase such as "In other words, you mean . . ." or "I think what you are saying is . . ."

4. **Remember that you are supposed to be listening, not talking.** *Silence* is key when listening. Don't be so anxious to hear the sound of your own voice that the speaker can't say everything he or she wants to. Don't concentrate on what you are going to say next, but on the speaker in front of you. By not filling a pause, you let the speaker know you are interested, and that your are expecting him or her to continue.

5. **Take notes.** Remembering what has been said in a particular conversation can be very difficult for a busy communicator with much on his or her mind. Take notes to help you remember what was said. It is courteous to tell the speaker that you will be taking notes to help you understand the situation.

Distractions to Listening. Internal and external distractions are too often part of the listening process. Knowing what they are can help you to reduce them and maximize listening effectiveness.

1. **Mental distractions.** Employees of GEI have very busy schedules. When an employee comes to talk, they may be thinking about a report that needs to be finished or preparing for a meeting or talking to a new customer. Stay focused! The person speaking to you deserves your undivided attention.

2. **Physical distractions.** A ringing telephone, materials on your desk, a siren blaring, or a noisy air conditioner can distract you from listening actively. Practice "selective focus." Put the telephone on call forwarding, set aside work that is on your desk, and concentrate only on what the speaker is saying, trying to block out everything else.

3. **Semantic distractions.** Semantics is the study of the meaning of words. Semantics also encompasses the study of linguistics. When the speaker's level of language is above or below you, when the speaker gives an excessive amount of detail, or when the person speaks too fast or too slow it is difficult to listen actively. When one or more of these occur, take steps to eliminate these distractions. Politely ask for a restatement of what was said, ask for clarification, or ask the speaker to slow down.

4. **Psychological distractions.** If you have strong political, prejudicial, or emotional bias about the subject being discussed, it will be difficult to focus on what is being said. Try to exercise emotional control. Set your biases aside. Recognize when you are "losing it," and redirect your energy to listening objectively to what is being said.

5. **General distractions.** Other distractions may inhibit listening such as:
   - Being disinterested in the person speaking or the subject being discussed, so much so you find it very difficult to focus.
   - Use of a monotone by the speaker.
   - Perception of major status differences between you and the speaker.
   - Poor preparation on the part of the speaker, or the speaker has little knowledge of the subject matter being discussed.

   Please take steps to practice and enhance your listening skills!

1. At a recent project team meeting, the project manager asked her staff not to drink coffee or eat food at their desks when there were customers in the office. Everyone agreed to this, but one team member, Pat, while not arguing the point at the meeting, continued to drink coffee and eat an occasional muffin at her desk when customers were present. She commented to another team member that she'd always done so and had never had any complaints. Other team members are starting to follow Pat's example. Is this a case of not listening? How would you solve this dilemma? Does Pat understand the full picture?

2. With the rest of your team, develop a "Two-way Listening Checklist," to be presented to the class as a whole. Include some active listening techniques and some internal and external distractions that take away from positive listening. Your boss will tell you whether this will be presented in class or whether a written report will be submitted.

3. Discuss what "listening between the lines" means. Why does a communicator have to know how to do that?

4. Your CEO may give each team an exercise to further practice active listening skills. This additional exercise will be given to you if the CEO requires it.

Organizing the Message Deductively

Before you begin to write for GEI, you need a plan—you need to organize. You need to get your ideas down in some sort of order. Fortunately, in business writing, several writing plans exist to help you plan and prepare a business communication. The following memo just came across your desk. It deals with *deductive writing*, which is a very common organization method in business communication. This organization method and *inductive writing* are the two most helpful plans for organizing your business writing.

GEI

12345 GEI Place	**Mt. Pleasant, Michigan 48859**	**517.555.1000**

TO: Project Directors

FROM: Larry Switzer, CEO

DATE: February 10, 200-

SUBJECT: The Deductive Plan of Organizing and Writing

Deductive Plan. The deductive plan of writing (sometimes called the direct plan) should be used when you expect the audience to be pleased or interested in your communication. Some estimates say that 70 to 75 percent of all writing in the office is deductive. The deductive plan consists of three major areas: (1) the objective; (2) the explanation, facts, and data; and (3) a courteous closing. You need to anticipate your audience's reaction to what you write and prepare your message accordingly.

Deductive writing may be used for the following situations:

- **Good news memos or letters.** Some examples of good news writing are letters of congratulations, letters of promotion, personal and business accomplishments, and any other good news you have to announce.

- **Favorable responses.** These are responses that a writer may make to some of the situations in the good news memos or letters section. For instance, you've received a letter of congratulations from your boss. Now you want to thank the boss for such a positive letter.

- **Order letter.** You need to order materials and equipment. You will write the letter in the deductive style. Also, if you receive an order letter, you may acknowledge that letter, also in the deductive style.

- **Routine inquiries.** Perhaps someone writes to your company requesting brochures describing a certain product you sell. You may answer that inquiry with a deductive-style letter.

- **Simple claim letters.** A claim letter is a request for a specific adjustment you want and that you think you are entitled to. Perhaps you ordered something from a company; and when the merchandise came, it was not what you thought it would be. Writing a simple claim letter will permit the company to make the adjustment.

Preparing to write a letter in the deductive style. Suppose you plan to write a letter congratulating one of your colleagues who has just received a promotion to associate sales manager. You know that Sarah has been a loyal employee to the company, she has worked hard for 17 years; she comes into work whenever asked, whether it's on a Saturday or a Sunday. She is helpful to everyone. She is fun to work with. You organize your letter (or memo) in the deductive style.

Step 1: Objective. State your reason for writing. That reason might go something like this: "Congratulations, Sarah, on your promotion to associate sales manager of GEI." That is your opening paragraph. The good news is stated in the first paragraph. You have used a deductive approach. Then you go to the next paragraph or paragraphs.

Step 2: Explanation, facts, and data. In this particular section, you give the reasons for your objective, or for what you stated in the first paragraph. "Your loyalty to the company and your willingness to work long and hard on any task you undertake is appreciated by all of us." All of this information could be placed in one paragraph; but if you have a lot of explanation, use two or more paragraphs.

Step 3. Courteous closing. Leave the reader with a pleasant, upbeat thought as you plan to close the letter. You might say something like "Best of luck to you in the future," or "Keep up the good work."

Job Responsibilities

1. Prepare an *objective* for each of the situations that follow:
   a. A simple claim letter. (Here's a little help: "Please refund $70 for the tickets I purchased for the Miserable Cru rock concert last Wednesday.") Now see if you can come up with some objectives for the remaining situations.
   b. A routine inquiry. You need some information from your travel agent for a business trip you plan to take to Cairo.
   c. A favorable announcement. Your company will celebrate Martin Luther King, Jr. Day with a morning seminar.

d. An order. You need to purchase file folders, staples, envelopes, and letter-head paper from your local Office Products Company.

e. An order acknowledgment. Someone has written you with an order for outdoor play equipment. Now you need to respond to the order.

2. Now, prepare the *explanation* step for each of the above situations. Assume any facts or information you need. Be prepared to read your work aloud to the other class members.

3. Prepare the *closing* for each of the situations. Strive for a positive, upbeat closing—one that will create goodwill between the reader and the company.

Organizing to Write Inductively

Lourdes Morales comes into your cubicle and says, "I just found out if we go with a different supplier on one of the *Mr. Mister* parts, we can save five cents apiece. This would save us over $15,000 in the next year.

"The bad thing about this is that the supplier we would be canceling this business with has been with GEI since our inception. They also supply us with various other parts for other items. I don't want there to be any 'bad blood' between our company and theirs. I'm going to draft this letter, but I want you to learn how to write these types of letters, too. I know this won't be the last time GEI will need to do something like this. It would be very helpful to me and to the entire company if you could become well versed in writing these types of messages."

Lourdes hands you the following memo on writing in the inductive style, which you now read:

12345 GEI Place	Mt. Pleasant, Michigan 48859	517.555.1000

TO:	Project Directors
FROM:	Lourdes Morales, VP Marketing and Sales
DATE:	February 9, 200-
SUBJECT:	Additional Tips for Organizing Your Writing

Inductive Style. The inductive style of writing (sometimes called indirect style) is used when you have *unfavorable* news to share with your reader. Some of the things that come to mind in this category are denials for promotion, firings, injuries or deaths, no raises, and others. The inductive-style plan is also useful for ideas that require persuasion, and especially sensitive news. The inductive-style plan exists to prepare your reader for the bad or unfavorable news, and the plan respects the feelings of the audience. The steps in the inductive style are (1) start with a pleasant opening, (2) give reasons for the news, (3) reveal the bad or unfavorable news, and (4) end with a courteous close. The main idea or objective of the message is delayed until you have prepared the reader for the bad news. In this way, the negative reaction can be minimized. Here are the steps in the inductive style of writing:

Step 1: Use a pleasant opening. Don't be too happy in the first paragraph since you are going to be relating some unfavorable news. Try to be as neutral as you can. A neutral or positive opening that does not reveal the bad news is called a buffer. Good news can be revealed quickly, but bad news must be broken gradually. By preparing the reader, you soften the impact.

Step 2: Discuss the reasons or give an explanation. Explain what caused the decision that made bad or unfavorable news possible. Be objective. Use nondiscriminatory and nonjudgmental language. Be fair. Show empathy. If a lot of reasons exist, you may use more than one paragraph.

Step 3: Reveal the unfavorable news. Be very clear in expressing the bad news. Avoid negative language. Don't be judgmental. State the bad news then go on to the next step.

Step 4: Close courteously. End on a positive and friendly note.

Job Responsibilities

1. Prepare an *opening* for each of the following situations:
   a. Telling the reader that he/she will not be rehired when the contract has elapsed.
   b. Your supervisor's mother passed away after a long illness.
   c. Your company no longer accepts credit cards for purchases over $5,000.
   d. The company will work on President's Day. Each year until now, your company has provided a holiday for President's Day. This year the union contract does not honor what they call "minor" holidays.
   e. You cannot refund the purchase price of a piece of playground equipment because the writer waited until after the warranty had expired.
   f. Only top managers may park in the restricted zone and then only in case of an emergency.

2. *Discuss the reasons* for the bad news that is coming up in the next paragraph, using the same situations as above.

3. Now *reveal the bad news* in each situation above.

4. For each situation, *close courteously.*

5. Get together in a team situation and discuss the different ways you completed the assignments.

You have just completed a short discussion of deductive and inductive organization in preparation for writing memos and letters. In further projects, you will get a chance to write memos and letters in both the deductive and inductive style.

Revising and Proofreading a Message or Document

E-mail messages, memos, faxes, reports, proposals, and other written communications require managers and employees to communicate their thoughts in writing, using the latest advances in computing. But no matter how quickly the writer wants the document to get to the reader, all written communication should be reviewed for accuracy before they leave the office. Turning out a perfect final product still requires the writer to *proofread* and *revise* every document, which means *more* than simply using spell check and a thesaurus.

GEI

12345 GEI Place   Mt. Pleasant, Michigan 48859   517.555.1000

TO: Project Directors

FROM: Susan Thomas, VP Human Resources

DATE: October 11, 200-

SUBJECT: Improving Writing Quality by Proofreading and Revising

Whether writing to a customer, coworker, boss, or senior manager, it is important that the document is as perfect as it can be. Since it is rare to produce a perfect first draft of anything, all written communication must be proofread and revised at least once before it is sent. Proofreading is reviewing the document for punctuation, typographical errors, spelling, grammar, format, and parallelism. Revising looks at the content in terms of conciseness, clarity, style, and organization. You can revise a document by adding material that was inadvertently omitted, changing and/or reorganizing part of the material, or deleting extraneous ideas to achieve conciseness.

Remember that you are representing GEI in any communication you have with others. Here are some important guidelines to consider when revising.

- Eliminate irrelevant information.
- Avoid generalities when you can be specific.
- Emphasize important points.
- Write naturally, avoiding stiff or pompous language.
- Do not use slang, jargon, or technical words your audience might not understand.
- Use bias-free writing. Avoid sexist, racist, or ethnic words or labels.
- Avoid excessively long sentences.
- Express different ideas in parallel form.

When proofreading, look for the following:

- Misspelled words. Use your spell check here.
- Typographical errors.
- Omission of words or phrases.
- Incorrect punctuation.
- Transposed or incorrect numbers, dates, or times.
- Incorrect capitalization.

Written communication needs to be correct on every level to be effective. If the message is disorganized and careless, GEI's credibility suffers. By taking a few extra minutes, employees can use these revising and proofreading suggestions to improve their writing skills.

Job Responsibilities

1. Using the information given above, revise and proofread the letter your boss assigns to you. This will be an individual project.

2. Work has been very hectic lately, so when your boss assigns a report to you, you ask a team member to complete it. When the report is done you proofread it and revise it, although the changes you make in it are minimal, because it was very well done. When you submit it to your boss, you take full credit for the work. Discuss the ethical implications of doing this with your project team. Select a team member to present the team findings to the rest of the class.

3. With your team, develop a list of problems or mistakes that can occur in writing when someone relies solely on the technology available to them when revising and proofreading a document.

Good News and Routine Messages

When we send information that will be viewed as good news or routine by the reader, it is usually organized in direct order. Such messages are usually the easiest to write when you remember the four C's of communication: Clear, Concise, Courteous, and Complete. Your memo today is from the Training Department in Human Resources. It offers you some techniques for writing a typical good news or routine message.

| 12345 GEI Place | Mt. Pleasant, Michigan 48859 | 517.555.1000 |

TO: Project Directors

FROM: Training Department

DATE: October 4, 200-

SUBJECT: Writing Good News and Routine Messages

Good news is always welcome, so it is important to present it in a positive way. The format for good news messages or routine message that will be considered favorable by the reader is as follows:

1. **Give the good news first**. The first sentence should give the reader the information that he or she wants to hear the most. Make it clear and concise. Leave out any unnecessary information. For example, if you applied to graduate school at Harvard and received a letter of acceptance from them, you would want the first line to read, "Congratulations! You have been accepted into Harvard's Business School." You would not want to wait until the last paragraph to read that news.

2. **Any additional information or details are given in the second paragraph**. Answer any questions the reader may have, and supply the details needed to make your

point. Continue to maintain your positive, upbeat tone. This section makes the message complete. The example in item 1 might talk about living arrangements or the semester calendar in this paragraph.

3. **Include a courteous and action-oriented close**. If follow-up action is required by the reader, say what is expected. An action-oriented close might be, "Please let us know your decision whether or not to attend Harvard by February 1, 200-." When no action is required by the reader, use the final paragraph to build a closer relationship with the reader.

When you are providing routine information, which is positive or neutral in nature, the same direct format is also used. Replying to a request for information, giving a refund, announcing a sale, or exchanging a product are instances when the direct format is used. If the routine message could be perceived as negative or bad news the indirect format is used. It is discussed in Application 13.

Job Responsibilities

1. Using the information given, write a letter to Mr. Duffy Clark, Facilities Manager, Bella Vista Condominium Development, 600 Sunshine Lane, Sarasota, FL 34200, telling him how and when you will be sending the 75 *Mr. Mister*'s that he ordered.

2. One of your team members has been named GEI's Employee of the Month. The CEO has asked you to write a memo to the employee notifying him or her of the award. Make any assumptions you wish regarding gifts or prizes associated with the honor.

 teamwork

3. As a team, critique the sample good news memo (see Example 9.1). Consider these questions: What is the objective of the memo? Does it achieve that objective? Does it follow the guidelines given in this project? What is the team's overall feeling about the memo as an example of a good news memo?

Example 9.1   Sample of a good news memo.

GEI

| 12345 GEI Place | Mt. Pleasant, Michigan 48859 | 517.555.1000 |

"A Leisure Time Activity Any Time of the Day"

TO: Larry Switzer, CEO
FROM: Wendy Wiltsie, Project Manager, Water Works Team
DATE: February 4, 200-
SUBJECT: Product Announcement

The new *Mr. Mister* automatic lawn sprinkler is ready for production. The attached report includes a marketing plan and specifications about the product. The Water Works team worked cooperatively to design and produce the *Mr. Mister.*

Prototypes of the sprinkler have been built and tested. Results of all the testing and consumer feedback have been exceptionally positive. Upon your review and approval of the enclosed information about *Mr. Mister,* production will begin immediately. We can have the first products available in the market place three weeks after production begins.

The team is very excited about the new product, *Mr. Mister.* We look forward to your feedback and getting approval to begin production. If you have any questions or wish any additional information, please call me at Ext. 1627.

Goodwill Messages

In the business world, not all communication is formal. Strengthening and building customer relations require a sincere, personal touch. There are also times when you want to acknowledge the accomplishments of fellow employees in a friendly, informal way. When a message has no specific business objective it is called a goodwill message.

Larry Switzer seemed in an unusually good mood at the weekly senior staff meeting.

"This has been a banner month at GEI. We've received two big orders from international customers. And, our national sales are showing a 7 percent increase over this same time last year."

"That's great, boss," Lourdes Morales replied. "I'm glad to see our promotions are working, and that our customer base is growing."

"Our work teams have all met their production deadlines," added Fareed Rajan. "I hope they know we realize how hard they have been working."

"To change the subject for a minute, boss," Susan Thomas piped in, "I heard the motivational speech you gave at the Rotary Club last week was excellent. An article in the morning paper quoted you and said you got a standing ovation."

"Thank you, Susan. It's nice to be appreciated."

After the meeting, the following memo appears in your in-basket.

| 12345 GEI Place | Mt. Pleasant, Michigan 48859 | 517.555.1000 |

TO:	All Employees
FROM:	Larry Switzer, CEO
DATE:	November 4, 200-
SUBJECT:	Letters of Appreciation or Goodwill

The objective of all GEI's business communication is to maintain or create as much good will as the situation will allow. But there are times when the message is sent only for goodwill. It has no purpose other than to improve the relationship between the sender and the receiver.

Typical messages of goodwill are:

1. **Congratulations.** When someone receives a promotion, receives an award, is named to a board, or elected to an office of a civic organization, it is always appropriate to recognize the accomplishment by sending a note. If you have a personal relationship with an employee or customer, you also may want to send notes for weddings, a birth of a child, or a graduation.
2. **Appreciation.** A large order from a customer, a referral to a new customer, or an employee who willingly has worked overtime on a special project deserve to be acknowledged with a letter.
3. **Condolence.** Notes of sympathy should be sent to an employee, customer, or supplier when they have experienced a loss, misfortune, or serious setback. These are often the most difficult to write, but they are often the most appreciated.
4. **Thank you.** A guest speaker, someone who does you a favor, or a contribution to a worthy cause deserve a note or letter.

There are a few guidelines to follow to ensure your message achieves its purpose of maintaining a warm relationship with the reader.

1. Be prompt, direct, sincere, and concise. Send your message as soon after the event as possible. Don't procrastinate! The direct approach is best even with notes of condolence. That is, state the most important point of the message first, next, give a few more details, and close in a warm, courteous manner. Sincerity and conciseness are part of all good communication.
2. Goodwill should be the *only* goal of the note or letter. A sales pitch is inappropriate in a goodwill message.
3. Don't exaggerate your feelings. "There is no way I can possibly express my undying gratitude to you," is probably not true. A simple warm, sincere thank you is much better.
4. Use a letter for outside correspondence. This includes a goodwill letter mailed to an employee's home. A memo may be used for interoffice messages.
5. In most situations, messages should be one page or less. Memos and letters may be typed, although handwritten notes are appreciated. Condolences should be handwritten.

Employees of GEI are encouraged always to thank customers for their business, and to use these suggestions when communicating messages of goodwill to customers and each other.

Job Responsibilities

1. Using the information given in the above memo, write a letter of appreciation to Mr. Ronald Perrott, Perrott Enterprises, Inc., 115 Baker Road, Albany, NY 12200. Mr. Perrott referred two new clients to you, both of whom gave you large orders.

2. As a team, write a form thank-you letter to be sent to all of your national customers. After the first draft is written, team members should proofread and revise it before the final copy is turned in to the CEO.

3. You have just learned that Kimeo Matsui, one of your most important contacts in Toyohashi, Japan, is about to retire. Write him a letter of congratulations remembering he is from a high-context country. The address is: Kimeo Matsui, Go Newa Machi, Toyohashi 4 Aichi, Japan.

4. You read the article in the paper praising Larry Switzer's speech given to the Rotary Club. Write a note to him congratulating him on his accomplishment.

Example 10.1   Sample goodwill letter.

January 20, 200-

Mr. Larry Switzer, CEO
Goodtimes Enterprises, Inc.
12345 Oak Boulevard
Mt. Pleasant, MI 48859

Dear Larry,

You were a big success! Thank you for speaking to us. The Rotary members who listened to your motivational talk last Wednesday thoroughly enjoyed it, and, in the process, learned something they can actually put into practice in the workplace.

Our members come from many different backgrounds and have varied interests. Often it is difficult to find a subject that interests everyone, but your topic, "Workplace Motivation," certainly did.

As you know, Rotarians have a social responsibility to become involved in issues and organizations within the community in which they live and work. You are a wonderful example of the positive experience that can result when that interaction occurs.

Sincerely,

Anthony Parrinello, President
Mt. Pleasant Rotary Club

Informative Messages

When you arrive at work today, the following memo is in your mailbox.

GEI

12345 GEI Place   **Mt. Pleasant, Michigan 48859**   **517.555.1000**

TO: All Employees

FROM: Larry Switzer, CEO

DATE: September 16, 200-

SUBJECT: Communicating Information

As employees of GEI, there are many occasions when you have to give information to people. It can be notifying customers of a new product, an improvement or change in the current product, or in answer to a request another project manager or your boss has made. While these messages may be sent in many forms (memo, e-mail, letter) the end result is the same—an informational report.

E-mail messages and memos include a subject line in the heading, but a letter usually does not. When sending an informational message by letter, it is best to add a subject line. It will look like this:

Lisa Perrott, Vice President of Sales
Landscapes by Perrott and Williams, Inc.
36 Montgomery Road
Clifton Park, NY 12065

Subject: Price change on *Mr. Mister*s

Dear Ms. Perrott:

If the news you are sending is positive or routine, the direct or deductive format is used. The majority of your informative messages will be formatted in this way. The deductive format is covered in detail in Application 6, but the main points are:

1. State your reason for writing.
2. Give any *additional* facts or information next. *Note:* Don't repeat information, just add details.
3. End with a courteous close, which may be action-oriented.

Occasionally, the information you are giving will be considered negative or bad news by the reader. For example, a customer's credit card is over its limit and you have to inform him or her about it. Here is a quick review of the inductive style of writing:

1. Use a neutral or pleasant opening. Do not give the negative information yet.
2. Explain the reasons why you made the negative decision.
3. Give the bad news.
4. Close courteously and sincerely.

This information is given to you to help improve customer relations through better writing skills.

Job Responsibilities

1. During the months of November and December sales for *Mr. Misters* usually slow down. Write a letter to your landscape and lawn care companies informing them of a 10 percent discount that will be available on all orders for spring received by January 10, 200-.

2. GEI has done a review of its health insurance expenses, which have been getting more costly each year. Although he regrets having to do so, Larry has decided to cancel the dental coverage portion of the policy. He has asked your team to write the memo informing all employees of this change in coverage.

3. Your job responsibilities include maintaining a safe work environment and staying within your budget. Both factors are reviewed in your annual performance evaluation, which determines the salary increase you will get. You have become aware of a potentially unsafe situation, which you know needs to be corrected. However, GEI is almost at the end of its fiscal year; making the needed changes now would put you over budget. Because you want to make sure you receive a nice raise this year, you decide not to inform anyone about the problem until the new fiscal year begins. Discuss the ethical issues associated with this decision with your team members. After the discussion, write a short memo to your CEO supporting your position on the issue.

Direct Requests

It has become apparent to the CEO that employees of GEI could benefit from knowing the correct way to make a direct request. Therefore, the following memo is circulated in an effort to maintain a high level of customer relations.

12345 GEI Place   **Mt. Pleasant, Michigan 48859**   **517.555.1000**

TO: All Employees

FROM: Larry Switzer, CEO

DATE: November 4, 200-

SUBJECT: Writing Direct Requests

Frequently you have to place an order with one of your suppliers, or you may need to request information about something, or you simply may be making a routine inquiry. You might want a discount on an order, or a replacement order for one that was sent in error. The request may go to another business, to a customer, or to someone in another department of GEI.

The best way to make these kinds of requests is to use the direct format, which was discussed in Applications 6 and 9. To review:

1. Ask immediately for what it is that you are requesting. Be clear and concise.
2. Follow with an explanation and additional facts so that the reader will have all the information he or she needs to complete the requested action. Be as specific as possible. It is helpful to give the date of your order or, when ordering something, state the model number of the product and the page number, if it is from a catalog. If you choose to send a copy of your order form or receipt, be sure to keep the original for your own records.

3. Use an action-oriented and cordial close. Tell the reader what action you expect him or her to take. If you need a reply in a certain time frame, courteously state it here. Asking for a reply also encourages your reader to respond promptly.

The tone of your request should be polite and cordial, even in those situations when you may be annoyed with the reader. You do trust the reader and do expect the reader to comply with your request and give you a favorable response, so be careful not to sound demanding.

To ensure a prompt and positive response from the reader, please use this approach.

Job Responsibilities

1. Place an order with one of your suppliers, Ted's Lawn Supplies, 5181 Gifford Lane, Chicago, IL 60600, for 5,000 sprinkler heads, Model #2716; and 10,000 yards of plastic nonkink garden hose, Model #71083. Ask that the items be delivered COD to GEI's plant in Mt. Pleasant, MI.

2. You believe additional education will help your upward mobility in GEI, so you have decided to begin an MBA program. You have heard, via the grapevine, that GEI offers tuition reimbursement to complete a bachelor's degree, but the company manual doesn't mention graduate work. Write a memo to the CEO, inquiring about the possibility of receiving funds from GEI so you can begin your graduate program.

teamwork

3. You frequently write letters of inquiry to suppliers with questions about parts and equipment you have seen advertised. Develop a form letter to send to these companies asking them to send you a catalog, a price list, minimum order quantities, and an order form for their products to your work team's address.

diversity

4. Adapt the form letter so that you can send it to suppliers in Japan and China. *Note:* You might want to review the information given in Application 4 before beginning this exercise.

technology

5. Your CEO just sent an e-mail to each work team stating that the vice president of finance, Fareed Rajan, has reported $50,000 remaining in the capital expense budget, which must be used by the end of this fiscal year or it will revert back to the general fund. Have a team meeting to decide what item you want to request. E-mail your request back to your CEO.

Unfavorable, Unwanted, or Bad News Messages

At times in your tenure with Goodtimes Enterprises, Inc., you will need to write a letter or a memo that conveys an unfavorable message to the reader.

The following memo came to you through interoffice mail this afternoon. A month ago, your team was asked by upper management to provide information on the credentials of Reginald Collins, a candidate for a high-level position at GEI. As you can see from the memo, you now have bad news to convey.

12345 GEI Place	Mt. Pleasant, Michigan 48859	517.555.1000

TO: Project Directors

FROM: Linda Matsui, Human Resources Department

DATE: February 22, 200-

SUBJECT: Writing the Bad News

Thank you for the information you provided for the promotion of Reginald Collins to the position of associate director of marketing research. The information you provided was helpful to us in making our decision.

At this time, we cannot promote Mr. Collins to the position of associate director of marketing research due to his lack of background in computer systems. In addition, Mr. Collins has several classes to complete before he receives his MBA degree from State University.

When Mr. Collins completes additional training in computer systems and when he receives his MBA degree, we will certainly be willing to take a look at his credentials again.

Because Mr. Collins is a member of your department, I would appreciate it if you will write a memo explaining the situation to Mr. Collins. Tell him that his application for promotion has been denied. Then send the memo to me, and I will edit it and send it to Mr. Collins under my signature. Writing a letter denying an employee request is good practice for you. In the future, you may be the one responsible for telling someone the bad news. Now, of course, it is my responsibility to express the bad news.

Please take care of this matter as soon as possible.

Job Responsibilities

1. Write the memo for Linda. Bad news is usually presented in an inductive format. Address the memo to Mr. Collins in the same way you would if you were actually sending the memo. Then forward the memo to Linda for her approval and for her to actually send the memo.

2. As an alternative to this assignment, select another member of the company and practice writing the memo through "live" dictation. (See the following instructions for dictating to another person or dictating to a recording device.) Even though dictation is not used as often as it was in the past, it is good practice for you to organize your thoughts and be able to articulate those thoughts in an oral manner.

3. Prepare another "bad news" memo to the employees of your department, telling them that this year, the usual one-day Presidents' Day holiday has been discontinued in response to this year's union contract.

4. Mr. Collins thinks he was denied a promotion once before with another employer for much the same reason as he was denied the promotion this time. In addition, the persons who were hired for the position were both women. Mr. Collins thinks that he was denied the promotion solely because he is a man. Discuss with your team members the entire situation.

Originating Letters Orally

Even though many executives do their own keyboarding, many of them still have another person to compose or keyboard the letters. In addition a person in sales may dictate to a recording device while in the car or away from the office. Good oral dictation helps one to organize thoughts and get those thoughts on paper. Here are some basic points to keep in mind:

1. Be ready. When you are answering a letter, be sure you have all the necessary facts and figures.

2. Tell the bad news inductively. Do not start the letter with a simple "You're fired." Give the explanation first, then lead up to the objective. Use the rule of primacy in giving the bad news. Remember, the rule of primacy says that the beginning of the writing activity gets the most attention. Therefore, lead into the letter with a pleasant thought.

3. Plan what you want the letter to say; jot down notes; outline the message, including the purpose for writing. If you are dictating to a recording device that will be used by someone else to type your letter, identify yourself.

4. Give the keyboardist all the necessary information: number of copies to be prepared; the recipient or recipients (sometimes you will want a copy of a letter to go to another person).

5. Do not be afraid to spell out names and places for the keyboardist. Give any special instructions you want completed, such as unusual format, a particular spacing pattern, unusual kind of stationery, or other out-of-the-ordinary instructions.

6. Speak clearly during the dictation. Apply the principles of clear and concise communication.

7. Request that the dictation be read back as you dictate, and especially after you are finished.

8. Do not sign the letter until that letter represents the best that your company has to offer. An incorrect or sloppy letter gives a definite negative impression of the company.

Writing a News Release

Companies and organizations write news releases to announce to the public new products or services, special events (such as plant openings, plant lay-offs, plant closings, company anniversaries, union contracts, management changes, or sponsorship of social action and/or cultural programs).

The purposes of the news release are both to inform the public about the company and its products and to create a favorable company image. Even the announcement of an unfavorable event, such as a strike, should try to present the company in a good light. Large corporations and institutions usually have their own public relations staffs or use outside agencies. However, a small company without a public relations staff or an agency will often want to give information to the public and will need someone to write news releases.

The following memo came to your desk today from Gloria Steinberg in the Marketing Department. Gloria is concerned that releases that go out from the company are somewhat uniform and represent the company in a good light.

| 12345 GEI Place | Mt. Pleasant, Michigan 48859 | 517.555.1000 |

TO:	Project Directors
FROM:	Gloria Steinberg, Marketing Department
DATE:	February 28, 200-
SUBJECT:	Preparing a News Release for GEI

We may have a slight problem at GEI. A team of state inspectors has begun an investigation of accusations that our firm has been using a hazardous substance in the plastic that is used to make many of our products. The inspectors have been to our Mt. Pleasant plant several times in the past two months. They have studied the materials here on site and have taken some of the plastic to scientific laboratories.

The Michigan Department of Environmental Protection preliminary report in the matter of Goodtimes Enterprises states in part that a "relatively serious pattern of usage of plastic material exists with regard to the production of recreational equipment. However, we need to look further into the matter."

For a period of approximately six years we have used the plastic with no one making any objection to it. We have been working within the guidelines of the Environmental Protection Agency (EPA). Up to now we have had no problems.

The newspaper got hold of the problem when several youngsters in several different states became ill after playing with toys made from the plastic we use. This is the first report we have ever had that anyone got sick. The newspaper published a report blaming GEI for the using an environmentally unsafe plastic.

After serious investigation by GEI, by the EPA, and by scientists we hired to look into the matter, we found that the plastic we have been using is not harmful. We are willing to use another material, but the material we have been using "is not harmful to people, animals, and vegetation," according to the EPA investigation. In fact, all reports are positive. However, the newspaper, we feel, is blowing the situation all out of proportion.

Please write a news release to the local newspaper explaining the entire situation. Your goal is to defuse the situation and get things back to normal here.

The following are GEI guidelines for writing a news release.

Guidelines for Preparing a News Release for GEI

The news release must be clear and concise and should be written with particular attention to the five *w's: who, what, when, where,* and *why.* Write the news release so that all critical information is in the *first paragraph,* information of the next level is in the *second paragraph,* and the least important information follows in one or more additional paragraphs. Editors must make your release fit the space they have available; if they must cut your release, they will delete the material *from the bottom up;* that is, they will delete the last paragraph first, and then the next-to-last paragraph, and so on. Be sure about the accuracy of your facts, and be careful to define any technical terms.

Type the release, *double-spaced,* on company letterhead. Leave the top third of the page blank for editors to make any necessary changes on the copy. Use 2- or 2½-inch side margins so the editor has room to list the changes. Begin with the place and date of the announcement. If the release is longer than one page, type *MORE* at the bottom of all pages (except the last). On the second and subsequent pages, type the page number at the top left. The page number is usually typed 3 or 4 times with a hyphen between so that attention is called to the page. At the right side of the second and subsequent pages, type a shortened title or description of what the article is about. Do not worry about having a perfect title for the article. The editor and those in the newspaper business will determine an appropriate title. Type *—30—* or *END* at the bottom of the last page.

Releases are usually sent to local newspapers, television stations, radio stations, and other special groups, such as trade publications or professional associations. Send the release to a specific person whenever possible. Otherwise, try to address the news release to a particular editor—for example, to the business editor or the education editor or the science editor.

See the following sample (Example 14.1) of a previous news release announcing our new vice president of marketing and research.

Example 14.1   Sample news release.

GEI

| 12345 GEI Place | Mt. Pleasant, Michigan 48859 | 517.555.1000 |

FOR IMMEDIATE RELEASE

For More Information Call:

Gloria Steinberg

GEI Enterprises

(517) 777-7777

MT. PLEASANT, MICHIGAN, MARCH 1, 200-. Mark
Williamson has joined Goodtimes Enterprises, Inc., as Vice
President of Marketing. Mark will direct the Michigan Sales
Office and coordinate the planning for an overseas plant.
Williams will travel extensively to the Far East while devel-
oping marketing channels for GEI.

Formerly, Williamson was director of services with International Marketing Associates, a consulting group in New
York. While at IMA, Mark developed a computer-based
marketing center that linked textile firms in the United
States, Finland, and Greece.

MORE

A graduate of the Columbia University Graduate School of
Business, Williamson is the author of *Marketing Dynamics*,
an informal examination of psychological appeals to the
buying public. The book has been used in marketing class-
rooms in several leading universities and in business training seminars throughout the United States, Canada, and
Great Britain.

Goodtimes Enterprises, Inc., headquartered in Mt. Pleasant,
Michigan, produces leisure-time equipment for use in
indoors or outdoors.

The company's main plant is in Mt. Pleasant, Michigan.
Additional plants are located in Albuquerque, New Mexico,
and Manchester, New Hampshire. GEI has been producing
leisure-time products for a number of years.

—30—

Job Responsibilities

1. Prepare the news release for Gloria's approval before you submit the release
   to the local newspaper.

2. Be prepared to *read* your news release to the news media. You may or may
   not be televised as you present the release.

3. After the reading of your news release, stand for questions from the media. Be prepared to give your answer "on the spot." Know the subject matter of the news release well.

 4. Work with other members of the company to see what changes may be necessary in the news release before you present the release to the public.

Instruction Writing

G EI provides instructions with all the products it sells. You need to provide instructions on how to use the product your project team has just developed. The following memo will help you learn how to write effective instructions.

12345 GEI Place	Mt. Pleasant, Michigan 48859	517.555.1000

TO: Project Directors

FROM: Keiko Mitsui, Human Resources Department

DATE: February 29, 200-

SUBJECT: Preparing Instructions

Please use the following guidelines for preparing instructions:

1. Instructions are written using the same three divisions that are used in most (if not all) writing:
   • an introduction
   • a body
   • a closing
2. The **introduction** provides basic information about the product, and answers the questions who, what, when, where, why, and how.
3. After the introduction, you will write the **body**, or the actual instructions. Instructions are usually enumerated for clarity.
4. The first sentence of each numbered instruction should begin with an active verb (such as *gather, place, pull, turn, remove*). Finish the instruction with additional sen-

tences; these can use an active or nonactive verb. Above all, make sure you tell the reader *exactly* what to do.

5. Instructions should be understandable by all who read them. Short, concise sentences help readability. Long, complicated words, terms, and phrases that are not easily understood by everyone should be avoided. You may wish to test the readability level of your instructions, which can be done on your computer.

    Note: If the product will have an international market, keep in mind American idioms that might not be understood by users in other countries. Also, people for whom English is a second language will better understand sentences that are short and clear.

6. Warnings or cautions concerning use of the product need to be given with each instruction as warranted. Think of ways the users could harm themselves or the product in the use of the product. Is electrical shock a risk? Should use of the product be avoided under certain circumstances? Is the product harmful or fatal if swallowed? If you answer yes to these or other questions that you ask yourself, warnings or cautions should be included in the instructions.

7. **Conclude** with a short closing (e.g., "If you follow all of these instructions faithfully, you should have years of use from your new blender.").

8. Have others read your instructions to see if they can follow them. Revise the instructions based on their feedback.

Now refer to the attached set of instructions for the *Wolverine Off-Road Machine*. Note that all three parts of writing exist.

Job Responsibilities

1. In groups of two or three, study the provided instructions for the *Wolverine Off-Road Machine*. Can you make revisions that will make these instructions easier to understand? Have any important points or cautions been left out? Rewrite the instructions and send a copy to your CEO for approval. Keep in mind that this product is sold internationally.

2. Customers are not the only people who will need instructions. Employees can also benefit from specific instructions. Write instructions telling GEI employees exactly what to do in case of a disaster, such as a tornado. Follow the same steps that you would for giving instructions for products.

3. Independent of your product team, write instructions for the product your team has developed. Follow the guidelines given in Keiko's memo. Compare your instructions with other team members. Merge everyone's instructions together into a final set of instructions for your product. How were the instructions improved by working in this way? Submit your final instructions to the CEO.

4. Lawsuits are common in today's society. Customers sue companies when they feel they are not properly warned of the dangers of using a product. A few years ago, McDonald's had to pay a drive-thru customer millions of dollars in damages after she burned herself on their coffee. Now McDonald's coffee cups carry a warning on them that says "Caution! Contents are VERY hot!" With your team members, visit a local supermarket or drugstore. Find and record at least 20 caution statements on product packaging. Try to find ones you consider funny or outrageous. Present your findings to the class. Discuss why companies might have considered it ethically important to put such caution statements on their products.

5. Take the instructions you have written for your product and have your computer test their readability. Readability is usually contained somewhere in the grammar function of a word processor. What is the average words per sentence? How many characters per word? Where does your document fall on the Fleish-Kincaid grade level? In general, an eighth- to tenth-grade reading level can be read easily by most people. Do you need to revise your document to lower the reading level?

Wolverine Off-Road Machine Instructions

Driving the *Wolverine Off-Road Machine* can be one of the greatest adventures ever experienced. With proper use and handling, your fearless driving can take you practically anywhere safely. Follow these instructions carefully before your adventures begin.

1. SECURE YOURSELF. Place yourself on the seat, making sure your feet are able to touch the operating pedals. Snap on the safety belt by pulling straps from above the head down to the belt lock, which is positioned between your legs. Make sure that each strap goes over each shoulder. The safety belt is secure when a snapping sound is heard when inserting into its lock. Place the *Wolverine* helmet on your head and secure it with the attached Velcro straps. WARNING: Failure to lock the safety belt securely or failure to use the *Wolverine* helmet may result in injury or death to the rider.

2. START THE MOTOR. Make sure that gearshift is in the parked position before starting the motor. Place your foot on the brake pedal and insert the key into the ignition. Turn the key clockwise (to the right) until the motor is turned on. Then immediately release your hand from this turning position. The running lights should be on as indicated by the green light on the dashboard panel.

3. DRIVE FORWARD. With your foot still pressed on the brake pedal, shift the gear into drive position labeled "F" on the gear panel. Release your foot from the brake and slowly press on the gas pedal using your hands to steer the *Wolverine* at the same time. Get used to maneuvering the off-road machine on your driveway or yard before exploring other areas.

4. DRIVE IN REVERSE. Make sure the *Wolverine* is stopped before trying to drive in reverse. Press your foot on the brake pedal and shift the gear into reverse position labeled "R" on the gear panel. The *Wolverine* will start moving in reverse when your foot is released from the brake pedal. You may accelerate, but reverse speed is limited for your safety. To drive forward

again, stop the *Wolverine* with the brake and shift the gear back into "F" position, or shift to "P" position to park.

5. TURN OFF THE MOTOR. To turn the motor off, simply turn the key counterclockwise (to the left). Never leave your *Wolverine Machine* unattended while the motor is running. When finished, remove the key from the ignition and put the key in a safe place.

The *Wolverine Off-Road Machine* was built for your enjoyment. Remember, for lasting fun, follow these safety instructions, and the *Wolverine* will take you on the ride of a lifetime.

Memos

A s the senior staff was leaving their weekly meeting, Larry Switzer stopped Susan Thomas and said, "I've noticed some of our employees are getting a little sloppy in their memo writing. Susan, will you please send out a memo that reminds our employees it is just as important to send a well-written memo as it is a letter?"

"Consider it done, boss," answered Susan.

The following day this memo appears in your mailbox.

12345 GEI Place   **Mt. Pleasant, Michigan 48859**   **517.555.1000**

TO: All Employees

FROM: Susan Thomas, VP Human Resources *ST*

DATE: February 26, 200-

SUBJECT: Writing Memos

A memo is the most common form of in-house written communication. Letters are sent outside the organization, but the memo is used for the internal exchange of information. Most memos are usually one or two pages, but sometimes the memo format is used for longer in-house reports. In today's technological world, e-mail is the medium used for sending many memos.

Memos can be directive or informational. They can transmit good news or bad news. The structure you follow in a memo depends on its content. The direct approach is used when the news is positive or neutral, and the indirect approach is used if the reader will perceive the news as negative or unpleasant. Regardless of the organization used, a memo has three major components: the heading, body, and the authentication.

1. **The Heading**. Memo headings can be in different formats, but the most common one uses the words, "To, From, Date, and Subject," as this memo does. It is the format that GEI uses for all its memos. The subject line summarizes the contents of the memo.

2. **The Body**. The body of the memo states the main idea. It holds the information you are sending to others. As in the body of a letter, the typed lines are single spaced. The organization of the information contained in the body will depend on whether the direct or indirect approach is being used. Be sure to summarize your message or request the action you desire at the end of your memo.

3. **The Authentication**. A memo does not have a complimentary close because your name is included in the heading, so it is customary to initial the memo next to your name. This is called the authentication. It verifies that you approve the contents of the memo. I have authenticated this memo by initialing by my name.

E-Mailing memos. When sending a memo by e-mail, it is not necessary to include a heading, because all e-mail programs automatically incorporate a heading of some sort. Usually, a function of the e-mail program allows you to send a copy of the e-mail to yourself, or save a copy of the memo, should you need to keep a record of the communication. E-mail programs also allow you to send messages to several people at once, making them especially convenient.

E-mail correspondence should be written in the same organizational format as other business messages. However, it tends to not be taken as seriously as it should, perhaps because it seems less structured (it lacks a "structured" heading, and you don't print out and mail the materials after you are finished). Senders tend to become extremely informal and use much less structure with e-mail. This lack of organization can cause miscommunication and other kinds of problems down the road. As an employee of GEI, make efforts to treat e-mail just as seriously as other forms of business communication.

Memo of transmittal. It is common to use a memo of transmittal when sending a report. The transmittal message usually includes highlights of the attached document, any comments that will stimulate interest in it, and an offer to discuss the report or assignment with the reader. The memo of transmittal is written in traditional "good news" format (see Applications 6 and 9). The example given in Application 9 is a good news memo that is also a memo of transmittal. Any reports you submit to the CEO require a memo of transmittal.

At GEI, memos are used for the day-to-day exchange of information. As in all writing, remember to be clear, concise, courteous, and complete.

Job Responsibilities

1. Lourdes Morales, vice president of marketing and sales, has asked you to contact retail outlets in your area to introduce your team's product to them, proposing that it be stocked in their store. To date, you have been successful. More than half the retail outlets you contacted want to sell your product, and orders are already coming in. Write Lourdes a memo giving her an update on your efforts.

2. Now suppose that 20 percent of the retail stores you have asked to stock your product have shown little or no interest. You are fairly confident you will not get shelf space at these stores. Write Lourdes a separate memo explaining the situation to her. What will your next steps be to ensure your product meets sales goals?

3. The CEO has instructed your team to write a memo to all employees telling them of the new "Employee of the Month" award that will be given to the employee who best represents GEI through excellent customer service. While he believes that all employees of GEI are conscientious in giving excellent service, he believes that this award will reinforce the importance of always putting the customer first. Be creative as well as professional as you create your memo: What are the rewards and incentives for becoming employee of the month? How will the employee be honored? What criteria must be met to be considered for the award?

4. Someone wrote a racial slur on the bulletin board in the employee lounge. GEI has a zero-tolerance policy for such behavior. The employee handbook states,

"GEI is committed to providing a workplace that respects the dignity and worth of each individual. It continually strives to provide an environment free from acts of discrimination and harassment on the basis of race, religion, ethnicity, national origin, gender, age or disability."

You have been asked to write a memo to all employees condemning the action, and telling them a Diversity Training Workshop will be held on Friday, July 23, at 2:00 P.M., in the auditorium, which all employees are expected to attend.

E-mail

This morning, Susan Thomas received an e-mail from Larry Switzer, asking her to conduct some e-mail training for employees. He indicated that some team members needed to be reminded how to use the company's e-mail system, particularly regarding "netiquette."

Susan wrote the memo in Application 16. She became particularly interested in the information on e-mail informality. The more she thought about it, the more she became convinced that many GEI employees are guilty of too much informality in their e-mail messages. She discussed the situation with Larry, who agreed that an effort should be made to help employees improve e-mail communication. As a result, Susan drafted and sent the following memo to the GEI product teams.

| 12345 GEI Place | Mt. Pleasant, Michigan 48859 | 517.555.1000 |

TO: All Employees

FROM: Susan Thomas, VP Human Resources

DATE: July 10, 200-

SUBJECT: Using E-mail

E-mail messages represent you and the company as much as any other kind of written communication. However, e-mail messages are so easily created and convenient that the writer sometimes forgets that e-mail must be planned and written as carefully as any other form of written communication. This memo offers guidelines for professional behavior when composing e-mail messages.

E-mail correspondence should be written in the same standard format that you use when writing memos and letters. The heading, however, is automatically supplied by e-mail programs and should not be typed.

E-mail can be direct or indirect depending on the information being communicated. It can be informational, persuasive, or provide good or bad news. As with all business writing, e-mail uses the four Cs:

1. **Courteous**. Begin with a friendly greeting; be polite. Select positive words to convey your ideas; avoid negative words, innuendoes, and accusations.

2. **Clear.** Place ideas in logical order so the reader can easily follow your train of thought. Use concrete terms whenever possible to enhance understanding.

3. **Concise**. Use as few words as possible, but also make sure you have included all the necessary information. E-mail works best when it is as short as possible.

4. **Complete**. Proofread carefully for typographical, spelling, and grammatical errors.

For more information on the four Cs, refer to Application 9.

Other guidelines. The following are additional guidelines and items of note as you communicate via e-mail:

- E-mail should only be one to two screens in length for ease of reading. If your message is longer, you should send it as an attachment. The body of an e-mail should then explain the reason for the attachment. Long reports and other lengthy documents should always be attached, never sent as the text in an e-mail message.

- E-mail messages can be sent to several people at once.

- E-mail enables you keep a record of the communication. You can save a copy of your e-mail, or even send a copy of the e-mail to yourself.

- Most e-mail software does not have a spell-check, so keep a dictionary handy as you compose your messages.

- All e-mail programs include a heading that lists *to, from, date,* and *subject.* The body of your message should begin one line below the provided header.

- Facial expressions and voice inflections do not accompany your message; therefore, you need to take great care in crafting your message to make sure it cannot be taken in the wrong way.

- Conclude your e-mail message with a "signature." A signature might only be your name. Other information you might add includes title, organization, address, e-mail address, fax number, Web site address, and telephone number. Some people also like to include a quotation in their signature. A signature should not be longer than six lines long, however.

Netiquette

Netiquette, shortened from *network etiquette,* is the term used for the proper standards of behavior expected from people who use e-mail. To use e-mail properly, heed these warnings:

1. **Never forget that a person is on the other end of your message.** When you are not face-to-face with the person you are communicating with, it can be easy to forget that the person is a human being just like you. Be careful not to say things you would not say in person, and take care not to damage the relationship or hurt feelings.

2. **Do not send anything confidential**. Electronic mail is not protected or private. Assume that anyone with a computer has the potential to read your message. Your employer can legally look at your messages if they feel they have just cause to do so. Hackers can easily access anything sent through the Internet.

3. **Do not tie up the network.** Compose messages off-line, save them, then log on and send already-completed messages. Also, do not send messages that are unnecessary or inappropriate. For example, do not send chain letters. Many Internet service providers and companies prohibit them. *Spamming*, sending unwanted email to numerous users, is also a frowned-upon practice.

4. **Do not send rude or angry messages**. Such a practice is called *flaming*. It is also considered impolite to type your message all in capital letters, because it is the equivalent of shouting.

5. **Do *not* read other people's e-mail**. Respect their privacy.

In closing, simply remember to write responsibly and that the person at the end of your message wants to be treated with respect. Follow the guidelines in this memo and you will represent GEI in a positive, professional way when using e-mail.

Job Responsibilities

1. Susan has asked each project team to prepare a list of what they consider appropriate and inappropriate behavior for e-mail and Internet use. She will ask you to share your list with the other teams so a master list of courteous behavior can be developed. What kinds of things do you consider appropriate or inappropriate? You might choose to research one or more of the various netiquette guidelines located on the Internet.

2. An announcement about a one-day seminar on "Handling Conflict in the Workplace" was in your mail today. You would like to attend. Send a request, by e-mail, to your CEO asking permission to go. Include all the necessary details for him or her to make a decision. Make whatever necessary assumptions you need to, so that your request is complete.

3. Susan wants to send out some more information on e-mail to the employees of GEI. She would like your help on the research that needs to be done. She asks you to use the Internet to find three current news stories on one of the following topics, and asks that you send copies of the stories to her with a short one-page memo that explains your findings.

e-mail privacy   spamming
hackers   flaming
netiquette   viruses sent via email attachment
company policies on e-mail behavior

Persuasive Sales Messages

When a new product is introduced by GEI, the word must be sent out not only to the press but to individuals as well. The information may be sent out by way of a sales letter. Sales letters are effective ways of getting information to people you know who would be interested in your product.

Mark Williams, a relatively new hire in the marketing department, stops at your desk this morning. He asks, "Can you or anyone in your department come up with an effective sales letter for our new product, *Create-a-Town*, an adventure play set and a learning tool for children from ages six to twelve?"

You respond, "I think I can do it—no, in fact, I know I can do it. Does the company have any guidelines for preparing sales letters? And I'll also need some information about *Create-a-Town* to use as a base to create the letter."

Mark says that he has all of this information available and that he will send it to you just as soon as he gets back to the office.

A few minutes later, you receive the following memo from Mark.

| 12345 GEI Place | Mt. Pleasant, Michigan 48859 | 517.555.1000 |

TO:	Project Director
FROM:	Mark Williams, Marketing Department
DATE:	March 2, 200-
SUBJECT:	GEI Guidelines for Sales Letters and Other Persuasive Messages

Here at GEI, we use a persuasive method called A–I–D–A:

A = grab *Attention*
I = establish *Interest*
D = create *Desire*
A = demand *Action*

Other methods for selling and persuasion exist, but we use this one here at GEI. Here is a short refresher that you might find useful.

- Capture the reader's *attention* in the first paragraph. Start with a question or a fact or a short story. Use lots of *you* attitude. Make the reader feel important. Keep the *attention* paragraph *short*.
- Develop the reader's *interest* in the product or service by describing what the product or service can do for the reader. Give facts, figures, and other information about the product or service that will cause the reader to want to read more of the letter.
- Create *desire* on the part of the reader to "really want" the product or service you are selling. Tell the reader what others have thought of or done with the product. Offer a guarantee, if possible. Tell the reader how much the product costs—but try not to make the price "stand out" from the other facts in the letter.
- Obtain *action* by telling the reader to act *now* to save money; or use a toll-free number, or 800 number; stress that the offer is limited. You will be able to come up with many good ways to get the reader to take advantage of your offer.
- Format the letter in a correct style. Here at GEI we let each department determine their own letter and punctuation style. Also, for this letter that may be sent to thousands of prospective customers, provide a fictitious name and address to see how the final copy will look.

Attached to this memo is a sample sales letter (see Example 18.1) so you can see the format as well as the approach used in the letter: A–I–D–A. In addition, the CEO may provide you with more illustrations of each of the four sections of the persuasive communication. *Take some time either alone or in a group to discuss the questions that appear after the sample letter.*

Information about *Create-a-Town*

Here is some information you might find useful when writing the sales letter I asked for.

- *Create-a-Town* is an adventure play set that encourages creativity while learning locations of important buildings throughout a town.
- It is a 10' × 10' carpeted mat with printed roadways, common buildings, people, cars—and anything else that might be included in a town.
- The play set is designed for boys and girls from ages six through twelve.
- Children will not only play in a realistic setting, they will also gain geographical knowledge.
- *Create-a-Town* can be set up just about anywhere.
- Children can arrange and rearrange the play set to resemble their town or any other town.
- Retail price is $199.
- The set includes cardboard buildings, toy cars, and other equipment found in a town.
- *Create-a-Town* is available for major cities in the United States. Play sets are available for Washington, DC, New York City, Los Angeles, as well as a wide variety of other cities.

Questions to ask about your sales letter

In writing an effective sales letter, you may want to ask yourself the following questions:

1. What was used for the *attention*-getting device? Would this device have captured your attention as the reader? Why or why not? What else can be done to get the reader's attention?

2. What was used to create *interest* in the product?

3. What technique or techniques were used to create *desire* in the product? Is an incentive used in the letter? If so, what is it? Is the incentive purely price-based?

4. What part does price play in the letter? Is the price properly placed so as not to call too much attention to itself, or call a lot of attention to itself if it is in fact a great value?

5. Is the call to *action* as easy as possible for the reader? What else could the writer have done to make *action* as easy as possible?

6. Overall, does the letter sound "exciting" to you? Would you want to buy the product? Why or why not? What else could have been included in the letter to get you excited about the product?

Job Responsibilities

1. Read the sample sales letter and answer the questions contained in Mark's memo in preparation for writing your own letter. What does the sample letter do well? What could be done better?

2. Write a persuasive sales letter for the new *Create-a-Town* play set, using the memo Mark gave you as a guide.

3. After you have come up with a draft of your letter, get together with one or two other employees in the company. Study all the letters in your team. Then come up with one letter that represents the team letter.

4. Check for what you may think may or may not be ethical statements in your press release. For instance, have you exaggerated some of the facts? Is the price a fair price? Can the price be lowered if the customer buys more than one set? Have you been honest in your facts? Will the reader feel that you are a trustworthy company? What will make the reader feel that way? Discuss in your team; then discuss with the entire company.

5. Save a copy of your letter for a future application. In Application 21 you will be preparing a print advertisement for the same product you just wrote a sales letter for.

Example 18.1   Sample sales letter.

12345 GEI Place   **Mt. Pleasant, Michigan 48859**   **517.555.1000**

March 3, 200-

Ms. Rachel Jiminez
9874 East Pickard
Canton, OH 45897

Dear Ms. Jiminez:

Get ready for a hot new toy that will drive kids absolutely wild with excitement! Goodtimes Enterprises, Inc., is proud to introduce to you the *Wolverine Off-Road Machine*—the latest and greatest in motor toy technology.

The *Wolverine Off-Road Machine* is an off-road, four-wheel motorized vehicle that offers hours of fun for children of ages seven to twelve. Available in gray with blue stripes, each car proudly carries the Wolverine logo on the side. The car's dimensions are five feet in length and four feet in width, providing ample room for two passengers. By including features such as a durable metal frame, a five horsepower engine, and a one-gallon fuel tank, the *Wolverine Off-Road Machine* has sped ahead of the competition by offering your customers' children the most realistic driving experience possible.

Not only is the *Wolverine Off-Road Machine* fun for the kids, but it is also worry-free for their parents. Due to features such as seat belts, running lights, and helmets (all included with each purchase), your employees can assure your customers of the guaranteed safety of this revolutionary new vehicle. Moreover, our engineers have included an adjustable speed control in the machine's design, allowing parents to monitor and set the speed up to a maximum speed of 15 miles an hour.

Your store can be the first to offer this sensational new toy to your local area. The *Wolverine Off-Road Machine* sells for a retail price of $350; yet, if you buy two or more, you may purchase them for $325 each.

All you have to do is to return the enclosed purchase order form TODAY, indicating the quantity of your order. If you have any questions concerning further details about this product, you may contact the following people in the Wolverine Division of Goodtimes Enterprises, Inc.: François Bakla, Julie Dunneden, or Rebecca Demeter.

Allow yourself this opportunity to be the first to market this exciting new toy in your area. Beat your competition by ordering your shipment of the *Wolverine Off-Road Machine* today!

Sincerely,

Mark Williams
Director of Marketing and Research

rf
Enclosure

Newsletters and In-House Publications

Companies large and small distribute special information to their employees through in-house publications. These publications range from inexpensively produced bulletins, newsletters, and flyers to high-quality newspapers and magazines. The readers of these publications are usually company employees and are likely to be familiar with many topics you might discuss in a publication. Employees usually look forward to reading the publication, often hoping their name or picture will be in one of the articles.

GEI publishes a monthly newsletter called *GEI Times* for its employees. Lucinda Puetz, current editor of the newsletter, has asked your project team to help in writing this month's company newsletter. She will be out of the office on family sick leave and desperately needs some assistance to publish the newsletter on time. You have agreed to help and are even looking forward to being involved. You received the following memo from her this morning.

| 12345 GEI Place | Mt. Pleasant, Michigan 48859 | 517.555.1000 |

TO:	Project Directors
FROM:	Lucinda Puetz, Editor, *GEI Times*
DATE:	March 4, 200-
SUBJECT:	Help!

Thank you so much for agreeing to help with the next edition of *GEI Times.* I am sure you will make an outstanding stand-in editor!

The newsletter is a collection of valuable information for both our employees and our clients. *GEI Times* always comprises the front and back of an 8½ × 11 piece of paper. This issue will also need to fit within that space. If you look at past issues, you will see all kinds of information included in the publication, such as a listing of employee birthdays, a summary of what's been going on in the company, announcements for future action, policy statements (our new smoking policy was one of them), and more.

I had begun to outline this month's publication before I was called away. I planned to include the following: (1) this month's birthdays at the company; (2) a reiteration of the smoking policy; (3) an executive summary of some of the projects your division completed, such as the news release, the development of our new *Create-a-Town* play set; and (4) a listing of vacation dates. This material, however, will not be enough to fill a front-and-back newsletter. The remainder of the material is at your discretion. Try to come up with something of interest to the company. You may wish to include the company's sexual harassment policy or its affirmative action policy.

For this issue of *GEI Times,* create a new nameplate or banner for the paper, such as a distinctive typeface or graphic on the top fourth of the front page. Include your name as editor on this edition. If you have co-workers help you with the paper, be sure to include everyone's name and title.

If this project is your first or one of your first times preparing an in-house publication, you might want to gather newsletters and publications from other companies, or look at past publications of *GEI Times.* This research should help you prepare.

Guidelines for In-House Publications

Here are some guidelines you might find useful as you complete *GEI Times.*

1. Keep the newsletter simple. Use words everyone will understand, and keep sentences and paragraphs short. Simplicity refers to design as well as writing. Clutter does not improve readability. Less is more!
2. Do not assume that the readers know everything. You should always give them enough initial information to orient them to the topic you are writing about before plunging into your assignment. Your job is to write to the readers of in-house publications in such a way that they understand what you say and are interested in what you say.
3. Be sure your written material is not offensive to anyone and is not just understandable—but unmistakable.
4. Verify information received from others. Print facts, not hearsay.
5. Use the graphic capabilities of your computer to give emphasis. Use whatever you feel the reader will find eye-catching, but still easy to read. Some examples of graphic capabilities include, but are not limited to:

Boldface	Large capital letters	Shading
Italics	Drop caps	Clip art
Underline	Multiple columns	
Left or right justification	Borders and boxes	

6. Use white space effectively. Leave enough white space around an article to make that article more eye-appealing.
7. Try for "catchy" titles to each article—not something necessarily "cutesy."
8. Proofread, proofread, proofread. Then when you have finished proofreading, proofread again. Mistakes in grammar, punctuation, other mechanics, and content reflect upon the company. Get someone else to read the materials. Remember that the spell-check on your computer isn't good enough. If you meant "and" but forgot the *d* at the end, the computer won't pick it up as a mistake.

1. Brainstorm with team members to plan the newsletter. Include the items Lucinda wants in the newsletter, as well as material you decide upon yourselves. Assign various duties to members of your team: Who will write which story? Who will take care of designing the newsletter on the computer?

2. Plan the layout for the newsletter. What graphic capabilities do you want to use? What do you think the new banner for the letterhead should look like? You might find it helpful to sketch out your ideas as you work.

3. Prepare the newsletter in a professional style using the computer. Your CEO will tell you whether you should make enough copies for everyone in the company (class).

4. Discuss with other teams the material they placed in the newsletter and their reasons for doing so. Talk about the differences in formatting as well. Who has used a two-column layout? Three columns? What other graphic elements enhance the readability or appearance of each newsletter? Also, compare and contrast the new banners that have been created.

5. Collect actual newsletters from companies in your area, or get on the Internet and find some company newsletters. After studying various newsletters, write a short memo to Lucinda suggesting some changes in future newsletters based on what you have found. Check especially for violations of ethical conduct.

Dealing with Company Layoffs

You have heard unsubstantiated rumors that company layoffs are imminent. No official word has been given yet. When you bumped into Keiko Mitsui from the Human Resources Department in the hallway this afternoon, she said, "Come into my office just as soon as you can." You are somewhat worried. No official word has been given yet, but you are sure the layoff rumors are what Keiko wants to talk with you about. When you get to Keiko's office, she hands you a memo. You accept it with shaking hands convinced that it is a layoff notice.

"You're probably really nervous about coming in here," she says. "I'm sure you've heard the layoff rumors. Unfortunately, they are true. Don't worry, though, you and your project team won't be among the ones being laid off. What I really need is some help from you and the rest of your project team in this delicate situation. The memo I just handed to you is what I've drafted for the entire company to receive in a few days. Please read it, then I've got something else to tell you as well."

Relieved for yourself, but also worried for people you know who aren't in your project team, you read the memo.

| 12345 GEI Place | Mt. Pleasant, Michigan 48859 | 517.555.1000 |

TO:	Project Directors
FROM:	Keiko Mitsui, Human Resources Department
DATE:	March 16, 200-
SUBJECT:	Justification Report of Company Layoffs

The Board of Directors of GEI met yesterday in executive session and has decided to implement a plan of structured layoffs in order to avoid cash-flow problems. Recent increases in oil prices, a critical substance in making our plastic, and rising costs of other materials have led us to a shortage of ready cash. Therefore, the Board of Directors has agreed that some layoffs are necessary.

The layoffs will involve only those recently hired, though some employees who have been with the firm as long as seven years may be among those who are laid off. Out of our total number of employees, we plan to name about 40 for short-term unemployment. They will be principally workers from the graveyard, or third, shift. These employees include assemblers, finishers, sorters, and other employees on the lower end of the wage scale.

Most of the employees will be out of work for a minimum of 90 days, perhaps as long as six months. The unspoken assumption is that we will get back on our feet in sales and cash flow and can resume our third shift sometime in the fall.

As you look up from the memo, Keiko says, "We're kind of keeping it hush-hush, but the board has said that we may well learn to live without some of these employees permanently. It would be possible to do the same amount of work with fewer employees. The company will do what has to be done, but will help the employees retrain or find new work. The board has agreed to help everyone fill out the proper paperwork to receive unemployment benefits, and we'll keep in touch with the unions every 30 days or so to let them know how we are doing. The union can, in turn, contact their membership.

"I would like for your project team to help in verbally breaking the news to the laid-off employees. It will be a tough job, but will also teach you a lot."

Just then the phone rings. Keiko asks you to please wait while she answers. "This should only take a sec," she promises. As you sit there patiently, Keiko becomes visibly agitated at some news she is receiving. "Okay, we'll tackle that one too," she says and hangs up the phone.

"Well, turns out I need your help with something else, too," says Keiko. "That was Larry Switzer. He just informed me that the media has heard of the layoffs, and they are suspicious of the company's motives. They have hinted that the company is in big financial trouble and that perhaps there will be even more layoffs and a plant closing. How they heard of the layoffs is beyond me, because it hasn't even been made public yet. But at this time there are definitely no plans to lay off more people, and there definitely won't be a plant closing.

"TV reporters from all the local stations will be stopping in to interview someone about the situation. Larry would like you to do the interview, because you have experience dealing with the press. In preparation for the interview, you should put together a justification paper, which fully explains the layoffs and the situation. Be prepared to read your justification for the layoffs to the local reporters who will, no doubt, converge on us in full force."

Keiko continues by telling you of two approaches to preparing justification papers: the modified inductive approach and modified deductive approach. You may choose either method that seems the most applicable for the situation.

The modified inductive approach contains the following information in order:

1. **Introduction.** Identifies the problem that exists and clearly explains it.

2. **Recommendation.** Proposes a solution or makes a recommendation.

3. **Implementation.** Explains how the recommendation should be put into effect.

4. **Conclusions.** Briefly states the advantages of adopting the recommendation.

5. **Justification of conclusions.** Explains why the conclusions are appropriate.

The modified deductive approach contains the following information in order:

1. **Recommendation.** Proposes a solution or make a recommendation.
2. **Primary justification.** Explains how to put the recommendation into effect.
3. **Implementation.** Explains why the conclusions are appropriate.
4. **Conclusions**. Briefly states the advantages of adopting the recommendation.
5. **Justification of conclusions**. Explains why the conclusions are appropriate.

Keiko says that she has attached a sample of a justification memo written in modified deductive approach (see Example 20.1) if you should need to see one. Keiko also reminds you that it is not common knowledge that the layoffs may remain permanent, and warns you that the media may ask questions about it. Keiko advises you to not reveal too much information while discussing the layoffs with the media.

Job Responsibilities

1. Get together with your project team. Brainstorm and discuss how you are going to inform the employees whose jobs are in jeopardy. Make notes. Then after you have come to some kind of plan, role-play the situation. One team member is to be the person who must give the bad news. The other members of the team will act as the employees. Be prepared to respond to any questions the employees may have. After you have done the role-playing, you should be ready to meet the employees face to face.

2. Prepare a short justification report to the media. The report should explain just what is happening in the company. Why the layoffs? Who is to be laid off? When? In preparation for reading the memo to the news media, read the memo to the other members of the team, who should be prepared to ask you off-the-cuff questions, the kind you may receive from the media.

3. Present your justification paper verbally to the media and answer the questions the media throws at you. Remember to not disclose that the layoffs may be permanent.

4. What do you anticipate will be the reaction of diverse groups in the company? Imagine that most of those laid-off are men, then imagine that they are mostly women, and finally members of a minority group. Discuss the entire situation in terms of diversity. How can the company be fair to all concerned?

5. Assume GEI would still turn a sizable profit if they kept the employees in spite of the rising costs. Do you think it is ethical for a company to lay off employees because prices have risen and cash flow is short? Think about the implications involved in this decision. Do you think employees will feel less loyalty to GEI, or be otherwise discontent with their jobs? Discuss your thinking with other classmates.

6. Think back on when you presented your justification paper to the media. How did you feel about withholding information regarding the possibility of the layoffs being permanent? Were you comfortable or uncomfortable? What do you think are the ethical implications of withholding this information? Write a short memo to Keiko regarding the situation you were put in. If you think it could have been handled differently, give specifics on how Keiko might approach the situation the next time.

Example 20.1   Sample copy of justification report (modified deductive arrangement).

TO: Roger E. Dodger, Human Resources Department
FROM: Project Director
DATE: March 17, 200-
SUBJECT: Override of Company Policy

Recommendation

The recommendation for Richard Thomas, one of our sales representatives, is that he be paid full commission on contract No. 38790, even though he gave the customer a special price on the windows. He should not be required to cover the price differential from his commission in this instance.

Justification

This exception is justified for five reasons:

1. Thomas made the contract adjustment in good faith, attempting to salvage a sizable account.

2. The evidence is cloudy. Thomas insists he told the customer that brown window frames cost 10 percent more than the white ones; the customer insists Thomas did not.

3. I have reviewed the sales closing procedure with Thomas, and he has demonstrated it to a group of trainees. I am convinced he will not repeat the error nor compromise prices unnecessarily in the future.

4. Thomas has experienced excessive medical expenses related to his child's illness. The commission is significant to him, but relatively insignificant to the company.

5. This action is an opportunity to demonstrate our faith in him and build the morale of a potentially excellent sales representative.

Implementation

The commission that he earned will be added to his next paycheck.

Conclusion

The decision should affect Mr. Thomas in a positive way. I feel that he will be more productive in his commission dealings in the future.

Justification of Conclusion

Mr. Thomas's work for the company has always been first rate. By paying him the full commission, his work will no doubt continue to be excellent. He is a valuable employee; we don't want to lose him.

Print Advertisements

Mark Williams from the Marketing Department saw you in the corridor this morning and flagged you down. He excitedly said, "I really liked the sales letter you came up with for our new *Create-a-Town* play set. That letter should do the job and bring us a lot of sales."

You are pleased that Mark is so happy with your work. Then he said, "Because you did such a terrific job, I wonder if you'd like to be involved further? I'm sending you a memo today that will ask you to prepare a print advertisement for promoting the *Create-a-Town* play set. We need to get this publicity to the media. I'm specifically targeting magazine advertising at this time. But plan the advertisement so that it can be used by other print advertising media as well."

You would love to do the print advertisement, and you tell Mark that you are looking forward to his memo. Later today, you receive the memo from Mark.

12345 GEI Place	Mt. Pleasant, Michigan 48859	517.555.1000

TO: Project Director

FROM: Mark Williams, Marketing Department

DATE: March 5, 200-

SUBJECT: Preparing a Print Advertisement

We need a print advertisement for *Create-a-Town*. This ad will appear in many leading magazines around the country. The print advertisement is a bit different from the sales letter in that the ad is not addressed to anyone in particular.

You have seen print ads in every magazine you pick up. That's what I want. I want basically the same material you used in your sales letter, but I want it on one page. The page can be reduced or enlarged in the magazine, depending on the price charged.

No need to set up the ad in letter format; you've already done that. You may wish to read the material I sent you for the preparation of your sales letter. That should answer many of the questions you may have.

Guidelines for Print Ads. The print advertisement is prepared using the same plan as for a sales letter. Again, use the A–I–D–A approach, but the guidelines are a little different:

1. Use all the resources available to you to catch the attention of the reader. Start with a good attention-grabbing headline. The headline should pique the interest of the reader, but it should be kept short. If it is too long, the reader won't even bother to read the ad. You may also wish to use graphics, pictures, bolding, underlining, capitalization, or other special effects to grab attention.

   Next, you have to write advertising copy for the ad. *Interest, desire,* and *action* should all be contained in the copy. The copy should be kept short to encourage people to read. Copy should be fun and engaging. You do not need to use complete sentences in the print ad; phrases will do; for example, "fun, safe, educational," or "excitement in your children's eyes," and so forth.

2. For the *interest* part of your copy, center on the one or two outstanding features of the *Create-a-Town* that you think the audience would like to hear the most. These features could be the same ones you used in the sales letter, or you could come up with a few new ones.

3. In the *desire* section, you need to convince the reader that he or she *must* have the product. You can use a variety of techniques in this section: a testimonial, a guarantee, a feeling that the best people own this product, and so on. Also, this is the section where you quote the price for the product or service. Remember that price, unless it is considered a bargain, is a negative. If the price is not a bargain, do not place the price in the first or last sentence; do not place the price as the first or last word of a sentence.

4. The *action* section requires reader response that is convenient and easy to do for the reader. Encourage the reader to come in to their closest retailer to buy, use an 800 number to order, or something similar. Some ads even have special sections at the bottom that the reader can tear off, fill out, and return.

Job Responsibilities

1. In preparation for writing the print ad, collect at least 5 ads from newspapers, magazines, and other printed sources. Critique them for A–I–D–A. Do they fit the bill? How do you think they can be improved? Write your thoughts in a memo for your CEO, and submit it with the ads.

teamwork

2. Brainstorm ideas for the *Create-a-Town* print ad with your project team. What will you do to grab attention? What will you include in the copy? What are the positives and negatives of the different things you could include in the copy (selecting this feature of the play set over that one, the different ways you could create desire, how effective varying calls to action would be)?

3. Prepare the print ad either in teams or individually. If possible, use the computer to do so. If not, use posterboard to create your ad. Use lots of color and other techniques that you used in the sales letter. Come up with an ad that people will want to read.

4. Bring one of the ads you critiqued in Job Responsibility 1 to class for discussion. Indicate on the ad what the ad maker used for the various sections. Was the A–I–D–A approach used? How do you know? What are the indications that this plan was used?

5. Find an ad in a magazine or newspaper that you think is particularly poor. Bring it to class and share it with your team. Rewrite the ad in a way that you think will be more effective. Submit the rewrite to your CEO.

6. Discuss the two ads you have brought to class in terms of ethical content. Look for overexaggeration on the part of the writer. Is the ad honest, in your opinion? Check out some of the other ethical considerations used, such as fairness and invasion of privacy. Then check the ad you prepared. Did you stretch the truth at all?

7. Research the Internet and the library to find out information on preparing a print advertisement. Report your findings orally to the other members of the company. What information will be the most useful to you in preparing the advertisement?

Example 21.1   Sample print advertisement.

LAWN CARE MADE EASY

Attention

Goodtimes Enterprises, Inc., is pleased to announce the newest advancement in lawn care: Simplicity.

Interest

Experience the future in lawn care today! GEI is thrilled to bring to you technology that has only been dreamed about until now. Our goal at GEI is to make life easier for all generations. We are confident we have accomplished this goal through the development of Simplicity.

Desire

Consider the time you'll save while your lawn is being mowed by Simplicity. Because it does all the work for you after you've programmed it, you can use your valuable time accomplishing more significant tasks than mowing the lawn. Simplicity is the perfect complement to all large-scale lawn care needs.

Action

Order Simplicity through our E-Z Lawn Care Catalog for the introductory price of $2399; but don't delay. Currently we are offering a special of only $1999 if purchased within the next month. If you want a sales representative to talk with you, simply call GEI at our 800 number: 800-777-7777.

Attention

Position Paper

When you arrive at work this morning, you received the following message from Susan Thomas in your in-box.

"I'm going to need your help," began Susan. "The media once again is reporting negative information about GEI. Yesterday's newspaper editorial covered a study performed by the Employment Study Committee. This story accused GEI of 'a longstanding bias toward minorities.' We feel the editorial was distorted and misinterpreted by the media. I can tell you what has been reported is simply not true. I have seen the ESC report; Linda Feldman, chair of the ESC, gave this report to me before it was made public. I was pleased with the work that had been done. However, the media, especially the local newspaper, seems to have blown the situation all out of proportion. Here's a copy of the editorial that appeared in the newspaper":

GEI CONTINUES GENDER BIAS
Mt. Pleasant—Goodtimes Enterprises, Inc., presents a continuing and pervasive bias in promotions in favor of white men, according to a recent study by GEI's Employment Study Committee.

Only eight women are in positions above that of Department Head. Further, none of the executive jobs, other than perhaps that of a general manager and several vice presidents, has ever been filled by a female.

GEI continues to employ a low percentage of females.

"GEI needs to prepare a position paper that will be read to the local news media. In fact, you will hold a press conference on the local television channel to present the paper and to stand for questions. Your work has been exceptional in the past, and Larry Switzer specifically asked if you might be able to handle this situation." Of course you can. Later that day you receive the following memo from Susan.

12345 GEI Place   **Mt. Pleasant, Michigan 48859**   **517.555.1000**

TO: Project Director

FROM: Susan Thomas, VP Human Resources

DATE: March 14, 200-

SUBJECT: Preparation of Position Paper for GEI

The news media is accusing GEI of continuous bias toward promotion of women. The media is basing this claim on a recent report made by the ESC, even though this report does not support the claims the media is making.

The ESC report stated that slightly over half (53 percent to be exact) of our employees are women. In fact, 35 women are in high-level positions at GEI. Ten of those women are vice presidents; one is general manager of the Outdoor Division, and one is the assistant to the president. In the past, a woman CEO headed GEI for four months while Larry Switzer was on medical leave.

Larry has gone on record, saying, "Our policy is that when positions become available, we consider *all* qualified candidates. GEI's long-standing policy of promoting from within remains firm. We go outside the firm only when no fully qualified applicants are available in house."

A position paper needs to be prepared for this situation, which will be sent to our constituencies: employees, management, shareholders, and the general public. Be prepared with the facts. You need to refute the arguments that appeared in the paper.

What Is a Position Paper? A position paper reports a corporate or company stance on some issue of interest to the company, the employees, and the public. The purpose of the position paper is to clarify, explain, or defend a company point of view toward a given issue. Position papers can be used to address a broad range of topics, some central to the business enterprise, others related to the business enterprise.

The writer of the position paper serves as corporate spokesperson, explaining and defending a particular viewpoint. The author of any business report, especially a position paper, must speak with a recognizably human voice to a human reader, protecting the integrity of all parties involved. The following lists the portions of a position paper:

1. **The Issue.** Describe the topic for consideration. What is the issue?
2. **Background/History.** Summarize the context for deliberation. The fact that there is an issue means that there is some background or history of the topic. Explain in detail.
3. **Various Viewpoints.** Survey the range of perspectives taken toward the issue. What have other companies done on this or a similar issue? Cite the sources in

your paper. The fact that others have had other similar situations may lend credence to your position.

4. **Company's Position.** State, explain, and offer support for the company stance on this issue. After you have studied the situation carefully and after you have seen what others have done, you are ready to state your company's position in this section.

5. **Discussion.** Analyze the merits and problems inherent in each perspective. Discuss how the position your company advocates answers the charges made.

6. **Summarize.** Summarize the entire paper in a few sentences or in a short paragraph.

Be prepared to read the position paper to the television audience. I have secured airtime on the local TV station; therefore, you must be prepared to answer questions thrown at you from the media after you have finished reading. Also, I want you to provide some documentation as to what other companies have done in similar situations.

Please submit the report for approval before you present it on TV.

Job Responsibilities

1. Prepare the position paper according to the guidelines given in the memo.

technology

2. Search the Internet to see what other companies have done in employment situations based on charges of bias or discrimination. Find at least three situations at different companies, and write a short report on what you have found. Be sure to include the name of the company, the date(s) the situation applies to, a brief description of the situation, and the conclusion (if the situation is not still occurring). Be prepared to talk about your findings with the rest of the company if required.

teamwork

3. Before you present the paper to the television audience, read the paper to others on your team to solicit suggestions. Incorporate any positive suggestions they may have.

ethics

4. What are the consequences of exaggeration by the media? Why do you suppose the facts were distorted or at least played down by the media? Is it too late to correct the impression that the media has established?

diversity

5. How might the position paper be different if the accusations made by the press were that GEI is biased toward Caucasians? How might it be the same? Write a short memo that summarizes your thoughts.

6. Call a press conference to read your position paper to the media. Follow up the press conference with questions from the media.

Introduction to Research

Although most of your writing on the job at GEI involves short memos, correspondence, and informal reports, there are times when you will be asked to research a topic to present in a more formal report, perhaps for the Board of Directors or top management people. The information provided in today's memo is to help you when doing the kind of research you will be asked to do at GEI.

| 12345 GEI Place | Mt. Pleasant, Michigan 48859 | 517.555.1000 |

TO: All Employees

FROM: Larry Switzer, CEO

DATE: September 16, 200-

SUBJECT: Introduction to Report Research

Research is the systematic and thorough study and investigation of a particular subject in order to gain information. Research is a necessary backbone to reports and papers; you must validate what you write or say with concrete evidence. There are two kinds of research data you may wish to use: *secondary* and *primary*.

Secondary Data Research

Secondary data consists of previously published research that someone else has collected and analyzed, and which is readily available for your use. The library and the Internet are two of the best places to find secondary data. Books, magazines, journals, newspapers, and government documents can all be helpful sources; which ones you use depend on your subject or project. The Internet provides hundreds of on-line databases, which are useful when doing research on business topics. GEI has access to two excellent sources for business and legal information. One is **www.lexis-nexis.com**. Students studying business, accounting, and law will find it especially helpful. The other is

ProquestDirect, which is a good source for journals, periodicals, and magazines. Its URL is **www.umi.com**.

Secondary research is often the fastest and easiest way to obtain information on a topic. It is far less time consuming and often the least costly way to collect data. You should check secondary research materials even when you believe you will also perform primary research because:

- Studying secondary data enables you to learn what information is already available on the subject, and can help you decide what structure your primary research needs to take.
- You might find that secondary data includes all of the information you want, and eliminates the need for primary data research.

Follow the three R's when using any secondary data sources in your research. They must be recent, relevant, and reliable.

1. **Recent.** In this rapidly changing world of ours, information can become outdated in a very short period of time. Do not make the assumption that because it's online, it's up to date. Most information on the Internet includes a date that shows when it was last updated. Refer to this date to determine the timeliness of the information. It is important to know when the supporting material applied and if it still does.
2. **Relevant.** Make sure there is a logical connection between the information you use from secondary sources and your project. Even if it is great article on the subject from a very reliable source, if it doesn't fit the specific way you are approaching the topic, don't use it!
3. **Reliable.** Is it a respected source of information? Has it handled the information in a responsible, non-biased way? For example, the *Wall Street Journal* is a very reliable business source, while the *National Inquirer* is not.

Primary Data Research

Primary data is research conducted to gather *new* information that cannot be found in secondary data sources. Primary data research can be more time-consuming and costly than collecting secondary data. However, it can be the only way to gather the information you are looking for.

Primary research commonly uses surveys and interviews to collect information. If you've ever received a call from a telemarketer who asked you questions to collect information, that person was likely conducting primary research. Even warranty cards you receive with appliances, software, and other purchases collect primary research through the use of a questionnaire. Experiments are also a form of primary research, but are not used frequently in business.

Interviews. If you decide to interview a person knowledgeable in the topic you are researching, use the following guidelines:

1. **Schedule an appointment for the interview**. Do not drop in unexpectedly. Explain why you want to interview the person and what it is you want to discuss. Most people are happy to talk about their expertise.
2. **Prepare for the interview**. Write out a list of specific questions to bring with you; make sure you will get you all the information you need.
3. **Practice your active listening skills**. Reviewing the two-way listening checklist your team created with Application 5 may be helpful.

4. **Take notes or record the interview**. This ensures that you remember details and answers correctly. Be sure to ask permission if you plan to record the interview.

5. **Use business etiquette**. Dress appropriately and be on time. Thank the interviewee when you leave, and ask if you can call after the interview should you need to ask a follow-up question. Send a thank you note.

Surveys. Another common method of primary research is the survey. Unlike interviews, surveys use standardized questionnaires to obtain information from a number of people. Surveys can be very useful when you need to find out information about or the opinions of a group of people. However, it usually is not possible to ask the entire group your questions. Imagine how time-intensive and costly a nationwide survey of the entire U.S. population would be! A survey enables you to select a simple *random sample* of a group in order to draw conclusions about the entire group. "Random" means that every person or item in the relevant population has an equal opportunity of being selected. Similarities between the information and opinions gathered are most likely indicative of the entire population.

A survey instrument must be *valid*, which means it must measure what it is intended to measure. For example, if you want to find out how many people own a particular type of car, you wouldn't ask what breed of dog they own. A survey must also be *reliable*, which means that if you were to repeat the survey with another random sample of the same population, you would get the same results. Validity and reliability are related. If a survey is not reliable, the results will not be valid.

Surveys can be conducted face-to-face, on the telephone, or sent in the mail. Designing survey questions can be difficult. To get useful information, questions must be neutral and nonbiased. It is best to get the help of an "expert" when creating questions for the survey and interpreting the data obtained from it. The CEO will help you do this, or will send you to someone who can. Keep questions as uncomplicated as possible. Ask only the questions you really need answers for. Most people lead very busy lives, and will only spend 5 to 10 minutes completing a questionnaire. The shorter your questionnaire, the greater the likelihood people will complete it.

Observation. This is a research technique in which you rely on your own powers of observation. When the data you want to obtain consists of an observable physical activity there are many ways to gather it: direct observation, or indirect observation, using a videotape or audiotape, when the subjects are unaware they are being observed. An example of this may be a videotape in a fresh fruit section of a grocery store to see how many people "taste" a grape or a strawberry. Mechanical observation may be used when accuracy is important, for example, how many cars travel through a busy intersection to see if a traffic light would help the problem. It would be difficult for a human observer to gather that data.

A good reason for using indirect or mechanical observation is the problem of reactivity. That is when the person(s) you are observing change what they normally do because you are watching. The main weakness of observation is that it only gathers external physical data. Feelings, attitudes, and other internal conditions can't be observed.

Focus Groups. A small group of consumers meet to discuss a particular topic or product. They are led by a facilitator, who "focuses" the group on the topic, and keeps them on track. They share their ideas, feelings, and attitudes about the product or issue. Many companies use focus groups because it keeps them in touch with customers' attitudes, especially about their products. Focus groups generate ideas about consumers' wants, needs, attitudes, and perceptions about a product or service.

Bibliographies and Citing Sources

A bibliography is a list that appears at the end of your report or paper that cites the sources you used or consulted in your research. A bibliography is often called "Sources Cited" or "References." When using secondary sources, you *must* give credit to the source and author of the original work. Citing sources involves including the name of the publication, name of the article or story, author name, date of publication, publisher, page number(s) the material is printed on, and sometimes even more extensive information. Even for primary data collection, you should include information that details how you gathered the information.

Many manuals are available to help you use the correct format when citing sources. The three most common styles used for citing sources are the MLA, APA, and University of Chicago documentation style. Your CEO will tell you which style he or she wants you to use for the research papers you write for GEI.

GEI employees are expected to be aware of the many ethical and legal considerations involved in doing research. Do not participate in *plagiarism*, the practice of presenting another person's work as your own. When you don't provide accurate documentation about the work of another person, you have plagiarized. Failure to acknowledge the source of even a few phrases, sentences, or paragraphs, whether quoted, paraphrased or summarized, constitutes plagiarism. Ignorance is not an excuse for engaging in plagiarism.

In addition, many materials carry a *copyright*, which means they are protected by the U.S. Copyright Law. Copyright gives the author or owner the exclusive right to reproduce, distribute, perform, display, or license his or her work. Copyrights can protect books, software, literary works, and even Internet pages. If you wish to use more than a few paragraphs from a copyrighted work, you often need to ask written permission from the author, owner, or publisher of the work. Once the permission is granted, it is still necessary to properly cite the work. You can learn more about copyright law by using a search engine on the Internet and entering in the words "U.S. Copyright Law."

Job Responsibilities

1. Do an on-line database search on one of the following topics and turn in to your CEO a list of the articles/sources you found, indicating which database(s) you used.

Sexual harassment in the workplace

Motivating employees

Marketing internationally

Technology in business

Improving communication

Marketing a new product

How many sources did you find? How did you narrow down the ones that were most relevant to the topic you picked?

2. With your team, select one of the many ethical dilemmas in business, and develop a survey on that topic. Your survey should be at least 10 questions long. Review the questionnaire with your CEO, and then survey 50 students on campus. Your CEO will give you specific instructions on how to select your sample. Retain your findings for a later project.

3. From the list of sources found in Job Responsibility 1, write a Bibliography for six of the articles, journals, books, or other on-line information, using the bibliographic style your CEO suggests.

4. Write a memo to your CEO comparing and contrasting two databases that you used when conducting on-line research. In the memo discuss which one you found to be most useful, and why.

Proposal Writing

L arry Switzer believes strongly in the abilities of his employees and encourages them to present to him any suggestions, or initiatives they have about company policies, new products, or research. Larry does ask that these ideas be presented to him in the form of a written proposal.

12345 GEI Place   Mt. Pleasant, Michigan 48859   517.555.1000

TO: All Employees

FROM: Larry Switzer, CEO

DATE: November 8, 200-

SUBJECT: Proposal Writing

The purpose of a *proposal* is to set forth a plan or intent. Business proposals have one common purpose, even though they have many different specific purposes. The objective of *all* proposals is to influence others—to stimulate actions that the writer considers good or desirable.

A proposal may be solicited or unsolicited. A *solicited proposal* is presented in response to a request for proposal (often abbreviated *RFP*). In the RFP, the requesting person indicates its needs, and the proposal writer attempts to show that the proposed plan can satisfy those needs.

An *unsolicited proposal* is initiated by the writer. That individual perceives a need or problem and offers a research plan, a product or service, or an action to satisfy the need. The proposal may be submitted to someone who is unaware of the situation. The writer's purpose is twofold: to convince the reader that a need or problem exists and to show how the proposed action will result in benefits to the reader.

Kinds of Proposals

Business proposals fall into three basic categories: proposals to investigate, proposals to provide, and proposals to change. Each may be used independently of the others. But the three may also be related to one another. The order in which the parts are presented must contribute to the reader's understanding of your planned investigation.

1. An *investigative* or *research proposal* is a formal version of a research plan. The order in which the parts are presented must contribute to the reader's understanding of the planned investigation. The presentation sequence should also lead the reader to appreciate the significance of the research.

2. A *product* or *service proposal*, sometimes called a *bid*, offers to provide a product to the recipient. These proposals are often solicited. The RFP usually specifies the content and format wanted by the receiver. To be considered, a proposal must follow those exact specifications.

    GEI uses relatively informal procedures to solicit product or service proposals. For example, any member of senior management may contact a project manager or work team, describe a training need, and ask for a proposal. In such a situation, the work team or project manager decides the proposal's content and structure. It must convince the senior manager that the team understands the need and can satisfy that need.

3. *Organizational or operational proposals* set forth suggestions or plans for changes in organizational structure or operations. Such proposals are sometimes called *justification reports* because a particular course of action is usually favored above all others and the report is written to present and support this action.

A Planning Guide for a Proposal

As in most business documents, it is best to ask, "What do I want to accomplish with this?" so, first state the *overall purpose or problem statement* of the proposal. Then consider the questions: Who, What, When, Why, and How?

- Who will read your proposal? Know your audience so you can address them in terms with which they are familiar. Are there other considerations you need to keep in mind?

- What will your audience be looking for in the proposal? Be sure to give them a statement of the problem, what benefits you can offer them, and any other information they need to respond to the proposal in a positive way. What method will you use to get answers to your questions?

- When will your product be ready? Or when will the problem be solved? Will you be able to deliver it on time? Will you provide them with a time schedule?

- Why does this problem need to be solved? Or why is there is need for this new product? Will you perform the major steps involved with creating your product?

- How will you solve this problem or create this product? How much will you charge? Are you going to provide a list of costs? How will you persuade your audience that this is a worthwhile endeavor?

    A proposal usually contains the following parts:

I. The Purpose or Problem Statement
    What is this proposal about?

II. Background
    Why do you feel this issue is important?

III. Procedures or Method to be used
    This section explains *how* you will investigate your topic, and *who* will benefit
    from it.

IV. Costs
    How much will this cost?

V. Work Schedule
    When the work will be done and completed.

VI. Summary

When these suggestions are followed, your reader is sure to give the proposal careful consideration.

Job Responsibilities

1. When on a trip to Japan to develop new business, your team's project manager is asked by Mr. Fumitoshi Sato from Toyohashi, Inc., to submit a product proposal, or bid, to provide his company with 3,000 *Wolverine Off-Road Machines*. The project manager knows that other companies with similar off-road equipment have been asked to submit bids, and also knows that in Japan, as in other countries, "gifts" are considered a normal part of doing business. In fact, Mr. Funitoshi has intimated that any bid that includes a "special gift" will get extra consideration. GEI has been trying to break into the Japanese market for months, but GEI's Code of Ethics expressly forbids the giving or accepting of any gifts that may be viewed as a "bribe."

    Discuss with your team the ethical issues involved in this situation, and then take a vote asking: Who would refuse to pay? Who would pay, but believe it was unethical? And, who would pay, but consider it OK to do in the context of Japan's philosophy of doing business? Share the results of the vote, and decide what course of action the team will recommend the project manager should take.

2. Your project team has been asked to submit a bid to the County Parks' Department for 5,000 *Mr. Mister*s. At the team's meeting to discuss how the bid should be presented, your Project Manager shows everyone an envelope marked "Confidential." The logo and return address on it are from one of GEI's biggest competitors in the lawn care industry. Your project manager tells you that it holds a copy of that firm's bid to the County for the same job, and he/she knows the information inside is genuine. Knowing what their bid is could be a big help to your team when preparing its own bid. Do you open the envelope? If not, what do you do? *Note:* GEI's Marketing Department often reminds project teams how important it is to stay knowledgeable about your competitors.

3. Using one of the following situations, prepare a proposal to be presented to the CEO in appropriate proposal format. Your CEO will tell you whether this is a collaborative or individual writing assignment. Topics for proposals are:

- GEI institutes a drug testing and drug awareness policy.
- GEI offers a child care program.
- Your project team is to be provided with individual PCs.
- GEI develops a new nonfinancial reward system.
- Your team develops a new product, the *Goodtimes Razor*.
- GEI considers opening a new subsidiary in Spain.
- Designing and publishing a monthly newsletter.
- Designing a GEI Web page.
- Conducting more in-house training program for employees about current workplace issues (for example, sexual harassment).
- Conducting a survey of employees to determine what they like and dislike about their jobs.

Using Graphics

On your desk this morning was a special memorandum from Erika Slough of the Marketing Department. Erika is in charge of writing and preparing advertising copy. From time to time, she initiates memos with helpful information for those who want to spice up their reports with graphics. Many writers use graphics to help in effectively communicating ideas in written reports.

12345 GEI Place   **Mt. Pleasant, Michigan 48859**   **517.555.1000**

TO: Project Directors

FROM: Erika Slough, Advertising Specialist

DATE: April 15, 200-

SUBJECT: Including Graphics in Your Reports

Graphics, when used properly, are extremely effective in communicating ideas in written reports. Selection of the proper graphic will help promote communication. You must know the basic purposes of graphic aids so that your report will be interesting and easy to read.

Graphic aids will help complement your report by summarizing lots of data into charts, graphs, and tables. Graphic aids will help identify your company through the use of aids. Appropriate placement and identification of graphic aids will enhance the effectiveness of your reports.

Selecting the proper graphic aids requires a basic knowledge of the purposes and design elements of the visuals.

Attached to this memo are suggestions for using the different types of graphic aids (see Examples 25.1–25.3). Here are some items to consider when using the aids:

Purpose	What is the purpose of the aids? Is the purpose to summarize? Inform? Clarify?
Placement	Where should the aids be placed? What are the appropriate locations? Within the text? In the appendix?
Identification	What are the various types of graphic aids that you can use? How are they referred to in the body of the text? How are graphic aids labeled?
Reader Benefit	Are there any ethics involved in using graphic aids? How can the readers avoid being deceived by the graphic aids?

To find material on graphic aids, look in your local library and look at the materials on the Internet. Also, thumb through almost any book or report, and you're likely to find samples and illustrations of the various types of aids being used.

Here are some DO's and DON'Ts when using graphic aids:

DO	Use graphics to support your major points.
DO	Tie your graphic to the text of your message.
DO	Place a graphic as close as possible to the text reference.
DO	Label, title, and caption your graphic clearly.
DO	Use graphics to help your reader visualize your message.
DO	Emphasize important points.
DO	Give reader's eyes a rest from the sameness of sentence after sentence.
DON'T	Hide graphics in an appendix.
DON'T	Try to put too much information on one graphic.
DON'T	Overuse graphics.

Job Responsibilities

 teamwork

1. With your team, use the library and Internet to find the many different ways to present graphics. Categorize them, and write a short report to Erika about what you have found.

 technology

2. Find an annual report from one of the Fortune 500 companies. Look in the library. Check the report for graphics. Are the graphics clear? Are the graphics understandable? Be prepared to present your findings orally to the other members of the company.

technology

3. Find some information on how to use computer graphics. Ask your boss to show you how to incorporate computer graphics into a report. Use the Internet and the library.

ethics

4. Create some data that you can use for graphics. Using the same data for all visuals, how many different ways can you present the material? Discuss your visuals with your team. Decide who has done the best job. Discuss the reasons you prefer one visual over another. Are any ethical considerations involved? Discuss.

diversity

5. Find an illustration of a company's organization chart. Prepare an organization chart for GEI. Present your findings as a team to the company employees. From the organization chart, can you tell if the company is diverse? Are women listed in the flowchart? What do you infer from the flowchart? Discuss.

Example 25.1   Tables.

A *table* is a graphic arranged in columns and rows. The table may be lined or unlined. A table usually displays words and numbers. A table has a title, short columnar headings that identify what is in the column, and sometimes a total. A table also includes a "Source," which means that if you have taken the information from another source or other sources, you must place that source at the bottom of the table. If the table is composed of original material, no source note is necessary.

MONETARY UNITS AND LANGUAGE OF SELECTED COUNTRIES

Country	Monetary Unit	Language
Australia	Australian dollar	English
Austria	Shilling	German
Belgium	Belgian franc	Flemish, French, and German
Brazil	Cruzeiro	Portuguese
Canada	Canadian dollar	English
France	Franc	French
Greece	Drachma	Greek
Japan	Yen	Japanese

Source: *American World Manual*, 2000 edition.

Example 25.2   Charts.

Three types of charts are used often in business reports: charts, flowcharts, and pie charts. These kinds of charts do not need lengthy text interpretation. An *organization* chart shows lines of authority among the various positions within an organization. An organization chart illustrates the relationships among departments and of personnel within the department.

Goodtimes Enterprises, Inc. (GEI)

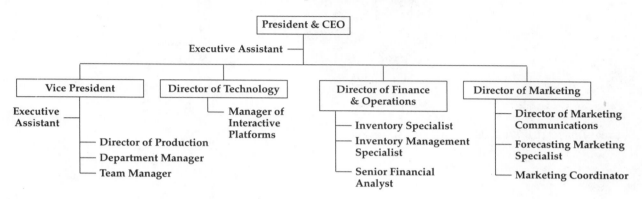

The second type of chart is a *flowchart,* which is used to illustrate step-by-step progression through a set of procedures. Steps could include how to complete a computer program, how to finish a task in an office situation, or how to manufacture or distribute a product.

Promoting Communication through Graphic Aids in a Written Report

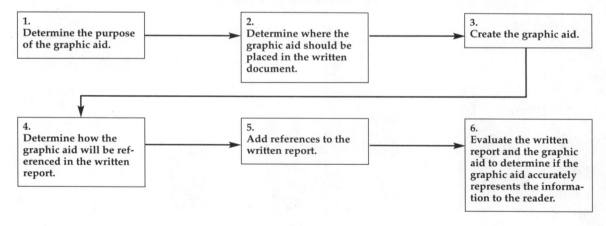

The third type of chart is a *pie chart*. A pie chart is used to illustrate how each piece of the pie relates to the whole. The pieces of the pie, starting at the 12 o'clock position, should be arranged in descending order of size.

EVERYDAY ACHES AND PAINS

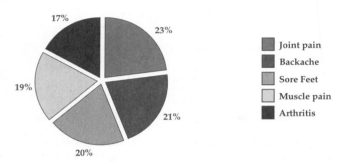

Source: *Time*, April 17, 2000.

Example 25.3   Graphs.

Graphs are drawings that represent the relationships of quantities or qualities to each other. A graph is an easy way to indicate a comparison. A *bar* graph is useful in comparing differences in quantities by the lengths of the bars. Bar graphs may be constructed horizontally or vertically.

QUARTERLY SALES BY REGION
(In Millions of Dollars)

A *line graph* is used to illustrate changes over time. A line graph can include either a single line or multiple lines. Trends can be effectively portrayed with a line graph.

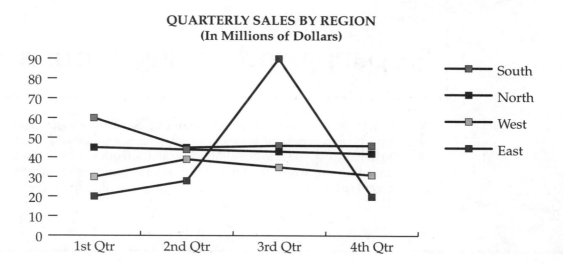

Preparing and Writing Reports

L arry Switzer expects his project teams to be able to write clear, in-depth reports on a variety of issues. If Larry accepts a proposal (Application 24), he usually expects it to be followed by an in-depth research report. As in all communication processes, the goal of the report is to provide information in a clear, organized, and concise manner. This memo will help you when writing reports.

GEI

12345 GEI Place   **Mt. Pleasant, Michigan 48859**   **517.555.1000**

TO: All Employees

FROM: Larry Switzer, CEO

DATE: November 8, 200-

SUBJECT: Preparing and Writing Formal Reports

The information provided in a report helps the reader make a more informed decision or better understand a problem. The report can also offer a choice of solutions or recommendations about a particular situation.

Formal reports are usually written in third person, while informal reports can be written in first, second, or third person (Application 27). When in doubt, or when doing business internationally, use the formal, third person, business report format, because it is more professional. Formal reports are classified by their uses.

Informational Reports. These are reports that simply provide information. Usually, no data analysis is given, and these reports generally do not carry recommendations.

Analytical Reports. An analytical reports gives an *analysis* of data. In such a report you will draw conclusions and make recommendations.

Research Reports. A formally written report presents the results of an extensive fact-finding search. It may make a conclusion or two, or several recommendations.

Organizing the Report. A standard format for organizing the report should be followed. This format is outlined below. Reports should *always* be professionally done on a word processor. Each section of the report should also be clearly labeled, and page numbers should be used. The preliminary parts of a report are described below in detail.

Preliminary Pages. A cover and a title page.

Memo of Transmittal. It is common to use a memo of transmittal when sending a report. The transmittal message includes highlights of the attached document, any comments that will stimulate interest in it, and an offer to discuss the report or assignment with the reader.

Table of Contents. The table of contents lists the report's topics by page number. You may wish to follow the table of contents with a page or pages listing the graphs, charts, or illustrations.

Executive Summary. The executive summary goes just after the table of contents. It provides the details contained in the longer report. It can be several pages in length, and is usually reserved for long, formal reports. It is, in fact, a short report of its own.

An abstract is one page or less, and is used for formal and informal reports that are up to six to eight pages. Both give the recommendations or conclusions in the report, and may state some of the supporting evidence. It is the one part of the report that is sure to be read by top management.

The executive summary or abstract should be *unbiased* and *factual*. It should be written *last*, after you have completed the entire body of the report.

Introduction. The Introduction of a report can contain some or all of the following.

Authorization and Background. At the very beginning of a formal report, you will have a short section that tells who authorized the report, and a little background information about how the project came about and why you are writing about it.

The Problem Statement. What is the problem or topic of the paper? A word that can replace "problem" is "topic." What is the topic of the paper? What are you writing about? This part of the report is sometimes entitled "Statement of the Problem." This is the section that tells your reader just what the paper is about. The statement of the problem should be clear and succinct.

Purpose of the Study. This section follows the statement of the problem. Why are you writing this paper or completing this study? What purposes will it serve? For example, the *topic* of the paper might be to determine whether or not GEI should open a subsidiary in Spain. The *purpose* might be to provide information to GEI's board of directors so they can make a decision whether or not to open a subsidiary in Spain.

Scope and Analysis. This section answers the questions *what is and what is not going to be covered in the paper.* Perhaps in your search to see whether or not your company is going to open a subsidiary in Spain you would want to cover the cultural aspect of Spain. Or, perhaps you are *not* going to cover the cultural aspects of Spain. This is the section where you explain what you are going to cover and what you are not going to cover.

Delimitations. Delimitations are the controls *you, the writer,* place on the report. You tell the reader what the study is delimited to. In the example above, you may delimit the study to the growth of business in Spain *in the last 5 years.* This is your decision as the writer. You will probably identify several delimitations in your paper.

Limitations. Limitations are factors over which you have no control. These are events that may occur just by the nature of the report you are doing. For instance, suppose you interview several people in a Spanish company. You have no control over their answers; they may or may not answer truthfully. This is a limitation—something that may happen and that you have no control over.

Methodology. The methodology section usually contains three subsections: *data collection, data analysis,* and *data presentation.* The *data collection* section is first, and describes how you obtained your data. Your will answer the following questions when determining what information to include in the data collection section.

- How did you get the information for the study?
- Did you use the library?
- Did you use personal interviews?
- Did you conduct a survey?
- Did you use the Internet?
- Did you obtain pamphlets from organizations?

The *data analysis* section tells how the data you collected was analyzed. Consider these questions when writing this section.

- How was the data grouped?
- Was the data interpreted statistically?

The third and last section of the methodology is the *data presentation* section. This section answers the questions:

- How will you as the writer present the data?
- Will you use charts and graphs?
- Will you use only narrative?

The reader needs to know the detail of the methodology of the report.

The Body of the Report. After the introductory part of the paper has been written, you are ready to present the findings in the body of the report.

The Findings or Body. Your findings should be presented in the body of the report in a way that makes them easy for the reader to understand. Organize the findings into related sections that flow logically from one to the other. The information contained in these sections, and the names of these sections, will be known once you have gathered all of your research. For instance, in the hypothetical study about Spain, you may group your findings into the following sections:

- Cultural aspects of Spain
- Concepts of time, United States versus Spain
- Do's and don'ts of gift giving
- Ethics, values, and laws

Present the findings only in narrative, or in narrative accompanied with graphics. Many people relate well to graphics but don't want to read the narrative in detail. Graphics also help the international readers understand the material more easily.

Ending the Report. The sections that will be included at the end of your report are the conclusions and recommendations, the bibliography, and any other material that supports your report, but was not logically placed elsewhere.

Conclusions and Recommendations. Based on the problem or topic being discussed, what did you conclude from all of this research? Did you meet the purpose of your study? If you were authorized to write the report by someone else have you answered all his/her questions? Conclusions may be written in narrative form or may be listed and numbered consecutively.

The recommendations are based on the conclusions. If you have concluded that Spain would pose too many hazards for your company, you may recommend that your company not set up the subsidiary in Spain. The recommendations must follow the conclusions. You cannot recommend something that you have not concluded.

Bibliography. The bibliography, which is the list of sources you used or consulted when doing research for the paper, appears at the end of the paper. Sometimes it is called the "Sources Cited" section or the "Reference" section. Many manuals are available to help you use the correct format when citing sources in the text of the paper and in the Bibliography (see Application 23 on report research).

Other Material. Pages that may follow the bibliography would be an appendix or appendices. An appendix is other information that you may or may not have referred to in your paper. Perhaps you wish to include a copy of the code of ethics of a company in Spain that you researched. It may be too large to put into the paper but you do want the reader to be able to see it if he/she wishes. You can include the material in an appendix. You may have as many appendices as you wish. Some writers include a copy of the proposal in the appendix.

Following these suggestions and format will help GEI employees write effective reports.

Job Responsibilities

1. Write a formal report. Your CEO will give the guidelines to you. You may use the topic of the Proposal you wrote in Application 24, or, with the permission of your CEO, one of the following topics:

   Any safety or health workplace issue.

   The contingent work force.

   Child care: whose responsibility is it?

   Do consumer protection agencies really help consumers?

   Ethics in the workplace.

   Marketing goods in a global environment.

   Labor/management relations in a global economy.

   The Internet and its effect on consumer buying behavior.

   E-commerce.

2. Project teams will do a report involving *primary research*. Each team should pick a topic on which they will prepare a short questionnaire or survey. The topic should be of interest to college-age students, and the survey should be one that can be administered and the data easily interpreted on a college campus. Prepare a proposal for your CEO. Once it is approved, collect the data, and write a collaborative research report on the results of your study.

Preparing Informal Reports

At times, Larry Switzer may ask project team members for reports about the work they are doing. While these reports should provide information in a clear and organized manner, they do not contain as many sections as a formal report and can be written in a more informal style. Today's memo discusses some of those reports.

GEI

12345 GEI Place   **Mt. Pleasant, Michigan 48859**   **517.555.1000**

TO: All Employees

FROM: Susan Thomas, VP Human Resources

DATE: July 10, 200-

SUBJECT: Writing Informal Reports

Informal reports may be written in first or second, or third person. Often informal reports are done in memo format. Remember, when doing business internationally, use third person, because it is more professional. Some of the informal reports you will have to do for GEI include:

Progress Reports. These reports are prepared for a specific period of time. If you are working on a study, your CEO may wish to be updated periodically on how the project is coming along and how much work remains to be completed.

An organizational plan for a progress report is:

- **Introduction.** This contains a brief statement of the background and ideas leading to the product or project, and an overview of the project to date.
- **Work Completed.** The "work completed" section provides all pertinent information about the present status of the product or project. When preparing a series of progress reports, this section can be divided into two parts:

(a) A summary of the work finished during prior reporting periods, and

(b) A summary of the work finished since the last report.

- **Work Yet to Be Completed.** This section is an overview of the remaining work to be done on the project, with target dates. It is here that an estimate is included of the final project deadline date.

- **Conclusion.** The concluding section of a progress report is optional. This section brings certain information about the goals of the project to the attention of the CEO or person authorizing the work. It might, for example, explain current or projected delays or cost overruns so that, if necessary, the reader can anticipate or make contingency plans.

Product Reports. A product report is a detailed written description of your product. Your boss may ask for a product report when the product is ready to be released into the market; or, it may be part of the marketing brochures that are included when the product is packaged. The following format is suggested for use by all GEI employees when preparing a product report.

- Tell what is the product; what it is used for; who it is designed for; and, the background of the product.

- Present the customer's need for the product by posing questions, citing examples, or suggesting a hypothetical case.

- Present the product in language, by numbers, and with graphics.

- Show how the product meets customer needs by experimental results, testimonials, or audiovisual displays.

- As in a sales letter or display ad, indicate the next step toward purchase, whether a toll-free telephone, fax, e-mail, or order blank. When possible give the name and address of a sales representative.

Special Purpose Reports. These reports do not fit elsewhere. These reports generally give a summary and present information. They may draw conclusions or make recommendations. An example of a report of this type of is:

- A written plan on how to recruit more women and minorities for GEI in the next two years.

- A report on the advantages and disadvantages of buying an existing building or constructing a new building for new office space for GEI.

- A "Justification Report" as discussed in Application 20.

A sample product report is attached to this memo (see Example 27.1) to aid you in your writing.

Job Responsibilities

1. Prepare a product report, in memo format, for your CEO. You may make the assumption that you are notifying him or her that the product is ready to be released, *or* that the information you are providing will be used in a marketing brochure which will be included with the product when it is released.

2. Larry has asked you to plan a half-day workshop for GEI employees on how to use Access and Excel, followed by lunch. You have to coordinate plans with the Information and Technology Department, get a caterer, and notify employees about the upcoming workshop. Larry has asked for a brief progress report, in memo format, on the status of the plans.

3. Larry has asked you to chair the annual company picnic. You have to find a location, plan the menu, design invitations, decide on the games, and buy the prizes. Larry has asked you for a report about the plans for the picnic.

Example 27.1   Sample product report.

Water Works, Inc.
6 Water Way
Mossy, ME 30076
Phone (516) 555-GROW
Fax (516) 555-WETT

TO: Mr. Larry Switzer, CEO
FROM: Sarah G. Perrott, Water Works Project Team
DATE: February 1, 200-
SUBJECT: Product Report

The new *Mr. Mister* automatic lawn sprinkler is ready for production. This information is presented to you so that we may receive approval to begin mass production.

The Product

Details of the *Mr. Mister* automatic lawn sprinkler are as follows:

1. It is a self-propelled sprinkler that comes preprogrammed to the dimensions of the buyer's lawn or with a remote control option. *Mr. Mister* can easily be transported around a yard or sports field for convenient watering.
2. It is shaped like a helicopter and equipped with a "pilot." The small passenger is a robot with laser sensors for easier maneuvering of the sprinkler.
3. The dimensions of the sprinkler are 14 inches wide by 20 inches long and 6.5 inches tall.
4. A variety of color choices are available; choose from red, orange, yellow, green, blue, or rainbow. It is a bright, very colorful item.
5. It operates on a 25-volt battery. The *Mr. Mister* recharge module is sold separately.

Development

Our entire Project Team designed the *Mr. Mister*, working cooperatively to design this easy-to-use watering product. The blend of materials with mechanical parts has resulted in a very attractive, useful, marketable product.

Prototypes of the sprinkler have already been tested in the lawns of team members and carefully selected focus groups. The result of all of our testing and consumer feedback has been only positive.

Schedule

Upon your approval, production of *Mr. Mister* can begin immediately. Approximately 3,500 products can be produced per week. The initiation of production within three weeks ensures that we can have the product on the market by March 7 of this year, just as the lawn care season begins.

Price

We are suggesting that the retail price of the *Mr. Mister* be $29.95, with three accessories sold separately. We are currently testing those accessories. You can expect to receive status reports on them within the next month.

If possible, we would like your feedback about the *Mr. Mister* product, by February 10, 200-. If you have any questions or are in need of any additional information in order to approve production, please call me at Ext. 2505.

Preparing a Long Report— International Study

Susan Thomas leaves you a voice-mail message saying that she has an important assignment for you. She tells you that the project will involve work in the international area. You are all excited, so Susan says, "I'll send you a memo describing the project and giving you lots of data that will help you complete the project." Later that day, a hand-delivered memo is given to you.

12345 GEI Place   Mt. Pleasant, Michigan 48859   517.555.1000

TO: Project Directors

FROM: Susan Thomas, VP Human Resources

DATE: April 15, 200-

SUBJECT: International Research Assignment

Your team, as employees of GEI, has been selected for an important assignment that will require that you travel outside the United States. You will accompany several other GEI teams along with me on a consulting project that will require you to be out of the country for approximately three to four weeks. Several different countries will be visited. Eventually, this consulting project will help us in expanding our plant to another country. But, we need to do this preliminary work first.

A large problem looms, however; no project member has anything but the most basic knowledge of the countries and their cultures. The knowledge you do have comes from high school and college geography or political science classes and from your knowledge of current events gained through reading the newspaper and other periodicals. Obviously, this information is not enough to carry you through three or four weeks of successful business and social interactions.

Your task it to thoroughly research one of the countries, together with its culture, and report your findings to all members of the project teams both orally and in writing. Your oral team presentation will be given on dates to be determined. Other members of the company will be invited to attend your presentation. Your written team report will be presented to the CEO.

The attached information (see Example 28.1) is a checklist for doing business abroad. Please research and report on the areas listed. Several suggestions for your research are listed under each of the items in the checklist. Your boss may decide that your team should research selected areas and another team research other selected areas.

Specific requirements for this project are listed as follows. The person in charge of the project may modify the specific requirements or may add to or delete certain areas.

Requirements

Country and culture	Your choice, but no two teams may report on the same country. We will decide in our planning session which country you will research.
Page length of report	At least ten (10) pages (double spaced) using 10- or 12-point typeface.
Format	Use a formal, third-person presentation. Include preliminary and appended sections; use headings and subheadings.
Proposal	Prepare a proposal for the study.
Progress reports	Two progress reports are required. Your director will tell you when they are due.
Documentation	Use mainly secondary data. Use the library and the Internet. Primary data in the form of interviews may be utilized. Try to interview a person from the country you choose.
Graphics	Include at least two (2) computer-generated graphics. Integrate graphics into the body of the paper.
Oral presentation	Each team will give a presentation of the completed research study. Time and date will be announced.

Example 28.1   Checklist for doing business abroad.

Checklist for Doing Business Abroad

Social Customs

1. How do people react to strangers? Are they friendly? Hostile?
2. How do people greet each other?
3. What are the appropriate manners when you enter and leave a room? Bowing? Nodding? Shaking hands? Other?
4. How are names used for introductions?
5. What are the attitudes toward touching people?
6. How do you express appreciation for an invitation to lunch or dinner?
7. Does custom dictate how, when, or where people are expected to sit in social or business situations?
8. Are any phrases, facial expressions, or hand gestures considered rude?
9. How close do people stand when talking?
10. How do you attract the attention of a waiter in a restaurant? Do you tip the waiter?
11. When is it rude to refuse an invitation? How do you refuse politely?
12. What are the acceptable eye contact patterns?
13. What gestures indicate agreement? Disagreement? Respect?
14. What topics may be discussed in a social setting? In a business setting? What topics are unacceptable?
15. Are there categories or a hierarchy in the social structure?
16. To what extent does a possible former colonial power still exert an influence?

Concepts of Time

1. How is time expressed?
2. What are the generally accepted working hours?
3. How do people view business appointments? View time in social situations?

Clothing and Food

1. What occasions require special clothing? What colors are associated with mourning? Love? Joy?
2. Is some clothing taboo for one's gender? What is appropriate business attire for men and women?
3. What are the attitudes toward human body odors?
4. When do people eat? How do they use their hands? Utensils?
5. What places, food, and drink are appropriate for business entertainment? Where is the seat of honor?

Political Patterns

1. How stable is the political situation? How does this stability affect business inside and outside the country?
2. How is political power manifested? Military power? Economic strength?

3. What are the traditional institutions of government?

4. What channels are used for expressing political opinions? Official government positions?

5. What information media are important? Who controls them?

6. In social or business situations, is talking politics appropriate?

7. What are the protocols individuals are expected to observe?

8. What influence do interest groups play in the company, and what effect do these groups have on the individual?

Workforce Diversity

1. Is the society homogeneous?

2. What minority groups are represented?

3. What languages are spoken?

4. How diverse is the workforce?

5. What are the current immigration patterns? How is workforce composition affected?

Religion and Folk Beliefs

1. To which religious groups do people belong? Is one predominant?

2. How do religious beliefs influence daily activities?

3. Which places are sacred? Which objects? Events?

4. Are minority religions tolerated?

5. How do religious holidays affect business and government activities?

6. What are the significant religious holidays?

7. Does religion affect attitudes toward smoking? Drinking? Gambling?

8. Does religion require or prohibit eating specific foods? At specific times?

9. What behavior is expected?

10. What are the differences between your religion and the religion of the country?

Economic and Business Institutions

1. What are the primary resources and products?

2. What vocational and technological training is offered?

3. What are the attitudes toward education?

    a. Do most businesspersons have a college degree?

    b. Do women have equal opportunity for an education?

4. Are businesses generally of one type?

    a. Are the businesses large public corporations?

    b. Are they owned or controlled by the government?

5. Is doing business by telephone appropriate?

6. Do managers make business decisions unilaterally, or do the managers involve the employees?

7. Do any customs involve exchanging business cards?

8. To what extent are foreign companies licensed to engage in foreign trade?

9. May funds or profits be removed? Under what conditions?

10. How are status and seniority shown in an organization? In a business meeting?

11. Are businesspeople expected to socialize before conducting business?

Ethics, Values, and Laws

1. Is money or a gift expected for arranging a business transaction? What are the legal, ethical, and business consequences of giving? Of not giving?

2. What ethics and laws affect business transactions?

3. Which is more important, competitiveness or cooperation?

4. What are the attitudes toward work? Toward money?

5. Is politeness more important than factual honesty?

6. How is a "friend" defined? What are a friend's duties?

7. What virtues are admired?

8. Is there a degree of freedom, or do either legal or governmental regulations intrude?

Communication Styles

1. What is acceptable in the area of verbal communications?

2. Are any gestures offensive?

3. What issues relating to time, space, dress, and manners are to be avoided to prevent mis-communication?

4. What examples are there for preferred style in written and oral communications?

5. Is the country a high-context country? A low-context country?

Languages

1. Is there one language or are several used?

2. What basic phrases should one know?

3. What are the polite forms of address?s

Education

1. What is the education of the persons with whom you will work?

2. To what degree does the country support education?

Some Additional Questions

1. Who are the country's national heroes and heroines?

2. What is the attitude toward gambling, drinking, narcotics, religion, and education?

3. What things are taboo in this society?

4. Which colors are positive in tone? Which are negative?

5. What are the special privileges of age and/or gender?

6. What are the important holidays? How is each observed?

7. What sports are popular?

8. What is the normal work schedule? How does it accommodate environmental or other conditions?

9. How will your financial position and living conditions compare with those of the majority of people living in this country?

10. What is the history of the relationship between this country and the United States?

11. Where are the important universities of the country? If university education is sought abroad, to what countries and universities do students go?

diversity

1. Each team will select a different country to research. The person in charge of the project will help you select the country. The purpose of studying a country is to see whether or not it would be feasible to expand a branch of GEI to that country.

2. Review the project on report writing. When this international research report is completed, be sure you have included at least the following items: (a) an executive summary; (b) a memo of transmittal; (c) a title page; (d) a table of contents; (e) a listing of illustrations, graphs, charts, or other preliminary pages; (f) the paper itself, including all of the sections you used in the report writing project; (g) a bibliography; (h) appendices, if necessary. Your director may include or delete any items.

teamwork

3. Oral presentation. After you have completed all of your research and have written the research paper, your team will be asked to present the paper to all of the employees of GEI. Plan your presentation to include graphics. You may be asked to use a PowerPoint presentation. Be able to answer any questions about the country you researched if you are asked.

technology

4. Use the Internet to find and interview a person from the country you choose for your research. Ask the person from that country some of the questions that appear on the checklist. Incorporate the responses into your paper.

ethics

5. Pay close attention to the ethical climate in the country you choose to visit. Send a memo to the project director of any ethical considerations that you find interesting or challenging.

Business Presentations

Larry Switzer notified his senior management team that they needed to be ready to present their department's quarterly reports at the next senior management meeting. After the meeting, he congratulated them on their presentations.

"Great job! Very thorough and well presented. The visual aids were very helpful, too. I hope all our employees realize there will be occasions when they will need to present information orally to an audience," Larry said to them. "It may be only one or two people, or it may be several. It may be inside of GEI or to an outside group. But, they must know how to do it well."

After the meeting, Susan Thomas decided to send a memo to all employees offering guidelines on their oral presentation skills.

| 12345 GEI Place | Mt. Pleasant, Michigan 48859 | 517.555.1000 |

TO:	All Employees
FROM:	Susan Thomas, VP Human Resources
DATE:	November 26, 200-
SUBJECT:	Business Presentations

A well presented oral presentation takes thoughtful preparation prior to facing an audience. First of all, you'll need to know who your audience is, and the circumstances under which you will be speaking, because this helps to decide what approach you will take. Ask yourself:

1. **What is the purpose of the presentation?** Whether the talk is to inform, to persuade, to entertain, to motivate, or a combination of those formats, writing a purpose or topic statement helps to define the parameters of your talk. It should be one sentence long.

2. **Who is my audience?** If you are speaking to members of your own team or department then you can answer this question yourself. But if you are speaking to another team or department, to visitors, or at an outside location, you will need to know whether you will be addressing managers, supervisors, or employees, and how large your audience will be. Knowing their age, gender, occupation, education, and attitudes and what they have or do not have in common helps you to more clearly define the purpose for the talk. Gather as much information as possible about your audience.

3. **What does the audience already know about the topic?** It is important not to speak above their heads about technicalities or details of an issue on the assumption they have a higher level of understanding of the subject than they do. Knowing the knowledge level of an audience helps you to present information that will enlighten and inform, sustain interest, and that they will understand.

4. **How much information can the audience handle?** The breadth and depth of your talk will depend on the knowledge level of the audience and how much time you have available. Tell the audience everything they need to know about your topic while staying within the time allocated for it.

5. **Where will the talk be given?** Know the layout of the room, your distance from the audience, whether it is an electronically enhanced room, and the type of lighting in the room. This will help you decide in what style your talk will be given, what kind of visual aids to use, and how large they should be.

You may be asked to speak with notice or sometimes without notice. If you unexpectedly are asked to speak at a team or company meeting, it is called *impromptu speaking*, which is speaking without warning or preparation. It is spontaneous and informal, and spoken without notes.

Extemporaneous speaking is when a presentation is planned and prepared. You use a few notes or follow an outline, sounding relaxed and natural. This is a very effective and a commonly used business presentation format.

Another type of presentation is *manuscript speaking*. It is a polished, practiced, completely prepared presentation read from a word-for-word manuscript. Government officials often use this style when giving a speech on television, reading from a TelePrompTer.

Memorized speaking is when the entire speech is memorized. There are no notes or manuscript in hand. This form of presenting is most commonly used by trained actors, and is not often seen in the business world.

Picking a structure for your topic is important. Using a structure that matches the topic will help meet the needs of your audience. There are several choices:

1. **Chronological**. This structure organizes the speech by events that occur during a natural progression of time. This structure works well if you are describing the development and history of something, for example, computers. Take each step or sequence in the event in the order of its occurrence and explain it.

2. **Classification.** This approach shows how a general topic is broken down into particular categories, subdivisions, or classes, for example, how many majors are offered at a particular college.

3. **Space.** The spatial structure shows the whole topic and how each part or substructure within that topic relates to each other. A diagram, map, or blueprint of what you want to describe is almost always used to support this kind of structure.

4. **Cause–effect**. This structure is used when you focus on what will or might occur when something happens, for example, if "X" happens, then "Y" will, or might, occur. The cause–effect style reasons that the presence of one condition brings about another condition.

5. **Compare and Contrast**. Discussing the similarities and differences of something, for example, comparing your product to your competitors, presents your message in a comparative relationship which aids in audience understanding.

6. **Problem–solution**. This method of developing the talk involves outlining a problem and all its consequences, for example, quality control within GEI, and presenting the solution(s).

7. **How to**. This is a process-oriented approach to a topic. Everything depends on what came before in this structure. Step 1 occurs before step 2, which occurs before step 3. This approach works well when the presenter is trying to teach the audience how to use something, for example, a PowerPoint program.

The structure that you choose must meet the needs of your audience by increasing their knowledge and enhancing their understanding.

Organizing the Presentation

A presentation is organized like any other report or form of communication. It has a beginning (introduction), a middle (body), and a conclusion, or summary. Before you begin the introduction, place your notes or outline in front of you so that you can follow them without losing your place. Check the audiovisual equipment and have your audiovisuals ready to go and convenient to use.

1. **Introduction**. This is when you get the attention of the audience, create the proper atmosphere, and state the purpose of your talk. Start positively and strongly. This gives the audience confidence in you. An attention-getter in the introduction is used to motivate the audience to listen to the talk and to understand its purpose.

2. **Body.** The two or three main points of your talk are given here. More than three may make it hard for the audience to follow you. Emphasize important ideas and show the connections between ideas. When necessary, reinforce ideas by restatement and visual aids. Use specific and clear language. Always let your enthusiasm for your subject show. Information should support the purpose statement.

3. **Conclusion.** End the talk on a positive note and as soon as you have accomplished your purpose. Do *not* introduce new information in the conclusion. Review the major points of the presentation and state your viewpoint and/or make recommendations if it is appropriate to do so. Give a clear indication that you are going to conclude, and then do it! There is nothing more frustrating to an audience than to hear a speaker say, "and in conclusion," and then have him or her drone on for several more minutes. Allow time for a question and answer period and thank your audience.

This three-stage approach will help your audience maintain their attention. The introduction gives them an overview right away, to see what points you are going to cover and in what order you will be presenting them. The body of the speech is devoted to the discussion of your subject, and the conclusion summarizes what you have said.

Helpful Hints

1. **Know your subject matter.** After you have gathered your research, review it and understand it thoroughly so you will be able to support what you have said in the question and answer period.

2. **Talk from notes.** Most business presentations are extemporaneous, rather than memorized or from a manuscript, *so don't read it word for word*. You want to be able to make eye contact with your audience. Present your talk in a natural, conversational style.

3. **Use visual aids.** A presentation supported by slides, demonstrations, PowerPoint, or other graphics increases audience attention. This is particularly helpful when presenting in other cultures. On the day of the presentation, check the room ahead of time to verify that all audiovisual equipment is in place and working.

4. **Practice, practice, practice!** Practicing helps you build self-confidence and get comfortable with your presentations.

Warnings

1. Use humor *only* if it fits and is appropriate. *Never* use off-color humor.

2. Do not move about constantly. This distracts the audience.

3. Do not lean on the podium, clutch it, or tap it.

4. Do not use slang or technical jargon the audience won't understand.

5. Do not stand stiffly like a tree. Stand in a relaxed, natural way.

Using these suggestions, you will get your message across effectively and with confidence.

Job Responsibilities

1. Your CEO will use the beginning of some class session to ask selected employees to do an *impromptu* talk. He or she may give you an idea for a topic to talk about for a few minutes or he or she may ask you to *think* of something. Your CEO will do this until all employees have had the opportunity to speak.

2. Team Presentations. All project teams must plan to give an *extemporaneous presentation* on one or two topics you have researched. Your CEO will give you specific instructions about the length of the talk and the kind of visual aids you will be expected to use.

3. Debating an issue is an excellent way to hone oral presentation skills. Debates present both sides of an issue to an audience, who may or may not be persuaded by one side or the other about the issue. Each project team will be divided in half. Teams may come up with their own current business topic from a newspaper or may pick one of the following:

- Is "whistleblowing" ethical or tattling?
- Should drug testing be mandatory for employees?
- Are sweatshops necessary evils?
- Is the term "business ethics" an oxymoron?
- Do flexible work schedules help employee productivity?
- Should affirmative action be eliminated?

Your CEO will provide you with the debate guidelines.

4. You have been researching the possibility of GEI instituting a flexible benefits program. These are programs that allow employees to develop individualized benefits packages for themselves by choosing the benefit options they prefer. While the program adds an administrative burden to GEI's clerical staff, and is difficult to implement, giving employees increased involvement in their benefits has been shown to improve morale, motivation, and productivity. You have to present your findings to GEI's senior staff. Write a *one-sentence purpose statement* to help you organize your presentation.

Oral Communication

Larry Switzer stopped Susan Thomas in the hall one morning. "You know, Susan, I may be worried unnecessarily, but with all of this new technology available to our employees, I don't want them to forget that one-on-one direct oral communication is still the most effective when dealing with customers and each other. Sometimes, I think they may forget the human factor in the communication process." As a result of Susan's conversation with the boss, you find the following memo in your mailbox.

| 12345 GEI Place | Mt. Pleasant, Michigan 48859 | 517.555.1000 |

TO: All Employees

FROM: Susan Thomas, VP Human Resources

DATE: November 8, 200-

SUBJECT: Oral Communications

Everyday you talk to fellow employees while working together to achieve GEI's organization goals. Communicating with each other is such a routine part of our workday that you may feel you have nothing more to learn about it. You may naturally assume that you are understood correctly and that you understand others as they want you to. But there are often barriers that block effective communication. Good oral communication skills require constant refining and improving.

All communication is a two-way process. It involves a sender, a message, and a receiver. Oral communication involves speaking face to face, the telephone, conference calls, or speaking to a group in a team meeting. It also involves nonverbal language: a smile and a nod can say a lot.

Nonverbal language, which is communicating without words, can reinforce or diminish the credibility of oral communication. The saying "actions speak louder than words" is very true. Cues, gestures, use of space, appearance, and body language all are part of the message you send. In our culture, when the nonverbal and verbal language blend well together, it supports and reinforces the message. You can also encourage a person to keep talking by using the appropriate nonverbal language. If the nonverbal language contradicts the verbal message the nonverbal message is usually the one to believe. People are careful to pick their words, but their nonverbal actions are usually done unconsciously, without thought. Vocal and facial expression, how eye contact is made, grooming, clothing, and posture are other examples of non-verbal communication that can affect the outcome of the message.

If you think your nonverbal skills need to be improved, pay more attention to your behavior and that of the receiver. Reviewing the tips given in Application 5 on listening skills also will help.

Feedback is another essential part of the oral communication process. It tells you how accurately your message has been understood. It may also show differences in understanding or disagreements, which can lead to ways to improve the way the information is given. While body language and/or verbal responses may provide you with all the feedback you need, asking the receiver of the message a few questions is a sure way to generate feedback:

Is there anything about which you are unclear?

Do you have anything you wish to ask me?

Did you find the information useful?

In order for real communication to take place there must be understanding. Use feedback to review the effectiveness of the way you send your message.

"Noise" is anything in the communication process that blocks, changes, or interferes with the intended message. In written documents noise can occur when grammar, spelling, and sentence structure are poor, or when the writer's vocabulary is above or below that of the reader. But in oral communication, noise occurs in many different ways:

1. **Physical Noise.** If there is background noise when you are talking with a customer or employee, it detracts from the message. A radio playing too loudly, a lawnmower directly outside the window, a siren, a noisy furnace, the conversation of others standing too closely, or the ringing of a telephone, makes the message more difficult to understand. When communicating orally, pick a quiet, comfortable place with as few audiovisual distractions as possible. Forward your telephone messages to voice mail to be retrieved at a later time.

2. **Physiological Noise.** This occurs when either the sender or receiver of the message has a physical problem that is interfering with concentrating on the issue at hand. Laryngitis, the flu, a stomach ache, or sleep deprivation are all examples of physiological noise. If you have planned to speak with employee(s) or customers on a day when you're not feeling 100 percent, it is important to try to stay focused and centered on your message to them.

3. **Perceptual Noise.** Perception is how you view and understand the world, or, how you "hear" what is being said. No two people look at the world the same way. That is, we all have a *subjective* view of the world, which affects how the message we are receiving is processed. Cultural background, experiences, attitudes, and beliefs influence perceptual noise. Some people will automatically trust people when they first meet them; others distrust people until they've gotten to know them. People in positions of power intimidate other people. Some people classify others because of bias, prejudice, or stereotyping. Try to be *fair* and *objective* in all communication,

remembering that every person is unique in his/her own way, and that hi[...]
perceptions are just as "right" as yours.

4. **Psychological Noise.** Process causes noise. Bias, prejudice, and stereotyp[...]
psychological noise as well as perceptual. Anger, love, or hate all block t[...]
open communication style that is needed to be a successful employee at [...]
you have strong political, prejudicial, or emotional feelings about the su[...]
discussed, it will be difficult to concentrate on what is being said. It is b[...]
someone else to speak to the person until you feel you can keep an open min[...]
ognize when you are "losing it," and redirect your energy to being objective.

5. **Semantic Noise.** The way we use words and language is called semantics. The most
obvious and severe semantic noise is in intercultural communication when two people speak different languages. Slang and jargon are also a barrier to effective communication if your audience is not familiar with the terms. Using words that are too
complex or too simple for your audience also can cause problems; so can being non-
specific in your language. For example, if you are conducting a performance interview with an employee who has a problem with tardiness, and say to him or her,
"You've just got to do better," he or she will probably not understand what is expected of him or her to improve. But, if you say, "You have been late three times in
the last 2 weeks and that is not acceptable. I will look at your tardiness record again
in 30 days to see if you have improved. If you have not, we will meet again to discuss
possible disciplinary action," he or she should understand clearly what is expected.

Words also have a denotative and connotative meaning. The denotative meaning is
the dictionary definition of the word, and the connotative is the subjective meaning that
has been attached to the word. For example, "inexpensive" means getting a good price
on something, but, "cheap" to some people, means, not only inexpensive, but shoddy.
"Teamwork" means to work together, while "conspire" also means to work together,
but on something bad or illegal. Before you use a word, be sure you know and understand both its denotative and connotative meaning.

The sound and tone of your voice, the listening skills of both you and the audience,
and the nonverbal cues you use can impact oral communication either positively or neg-
atively. The following suggestions are to help you get your message across in the most
positive manner.

1. Plan what you want to say. Think about the purpose of the talk. Know what it is that
you want to accomplish. Be specific. Don't stray from the message you want to deliver.

2. Use pauses, expression, and voice tone to add emphasis to stress important points.

3. Speak slowly. When you speak too quickly it diminishes your message.

4. Stay focused. The person(s) in front of you deserves your undivided attention. A
review of Application 5 on listening skills would be helpful, because for oral communication to be effective, listening is required.

5. Maintain emotional control. Put your biases aside.

6. Maintain a friendly, open demeanor. Use the nonverbal cues of eye contact and
leaning toward your audience to show empathy. It has great value in project teams
and in workplace situations in general.

7. *Always* ask for feedback to clear up any questions or confusion immediately. This
allows you the opportunity to provide additional information if it is needed.

8. Summarize what has been said, and review key points. Offer the opportunity for a
follow-up talk if it would add to maintaining positive employee relations.

These suggestions are offered to help employees reduce barriers to communication
at GEI. Communicating clearly should be an ongoing objective of all GEI project teams.

1. Each student will give a 2- to 3-minute oral talk about himself or herself. Use simple conversational language, telling the other project teams about your work experience, your educational experience (colleges or high schools you have attended), any special skills you have, and hobbies, extracurricular activities, or sports you enjoy. The CEO will allow time for a question and answer period at the end of your talk.

diversity

2. Slang and jargon cause noise in the communication process. A few commonly used expressions that we hear often are:

Wild goose chase	One for the road	Dead in the water
Catch your breath	A ballpark figure	Off the wall
Down and dirty	Don't reinvent the wheel	Shoot from the hip

Each team will now add to this list of expressions. Compile a long list and turn it in to your CEO. Then the CEO will give each project team a partial list of the terms and divide the teams in half. Half of the team will be assigned a foreign country in which they supposedly live. They speak English, but they have only been in this country a short time, so they don't understand these expressions. It is up to the other half of the team to explain to them what the terms mean in clear, simple, specific language.

3. This is an exercise in perceptual differences. Your CEO will write three questions on the board for each employee to answer. He or she will collect the answers. (You do not have to sign your name.) The CEO will list the variety of answers on the board under each question, and open the floor for discussion about why there is such a variety among all of your answers when so many of you seem to come from similar backgrounds.

Meeting Skills

In today's business world, a need exists for interchange of ideas, for mutual understandings, and for decision making based on many points of view. Effective meetings must be planned as well as recorded for future reference. A knowledge of parliamentary procedures is vital to anyone involved in meetings.

Caroline Crinole, office manager of the Human Resources Department, stops by your office and says: "You know, we have lots of meetings here at GEI—meetings that take place almost every day. You will be involved in many meetings during your time at GEI. So, you need to learn how to plan for a meeting by preparing an agenda, as well as recording the proceedings of meetings with the minutes."

"At GEI," Caroline continues, "we don't assign the task of taking minutes to just one person—we spread the task among many employees. I need one of the project directors to take minutes at a meeting that will be coming up next week. You need to be prepared, however, because GEI has a set procedure for taking minutes.

"Okay, but do you have any materials that I might use to become acquainted with preparing an agenda and minutes?" you ask. Caroline says she does and that she will send you a memo with attachments that shows how to prepare the materials (see Example 31.1). The memo arrives later that day.

| 12345 GEI Place | Mt. Pleasant, Michigan 48859 | 517.555.1000 |

TO: Project Director

FROM: Caroline Crinole, Office Manager

DATE: April 1, 200-

SUBJECT: Preparation of Agenda and Minutes for GEI

The following procedure is used at GEI for successful meetings: preparing before the meeting; developing an agenda; running the meeting successfully; and recording the minutes.

1. **Preparing Before the Meeting.** There are some questions you should ask yourself to become fully prepared for a meeting. Often, the answers to some or all of these

questions may be distributed to attendees before the actual meeting, so everyone comes to the meeting with the same knowledge and expectations.

- **Who?** Do all members of the team need to be at the meeting? Who is present? Be sure you know who is coming even though all persons do not show up.
- **What?** What is the purpose or objective of the meeting? Keep the purpose of the meeting clearly in your mind before you prepare the agenda.
- **Where?** Where will the meeting be held? Is the location convenient to the majority of participants? If you have the task of selecting a meeting room, keep the convenience factor clearly in mind.
- **When?** What time is most convenient for participants? What days? When announcing the meeting, give participants the *starting* and *ending* times so they can block out the time that is needed to give the meeting their full attention.
- **Why?** Is this meeting *really* necessary? Do not waste team members' time. If the meeting is to solve a problem, disseminate information, give a product update, or to collaborate on an assignment, know what you want to accomplish.

2. **Developing an Agenda**. An agenda simply identifies the topics to be discussed in the meeting. Prepare the agenda ahead of time and see that each attendee has a copy of the agenda well ahead of the meeting date. An agenda is sometimes called an "Order of Business." The following is a typical order of business for standard meetings:

- Call to order by the presiding officer
- Roll call
- Minutes of the previous meeting
- Treasurer's report
- Reading of correspondence
- Committee reports
- Unfinished business
- New business
- Announcements (sometimes appear after the call to order)
- Adjournment

3. **Running a Meeting.** There are many hints and tips for running a successful meeting, not all of which are covered here. However, the following are some of the most important things to keep in mind while running a meeting.

Beginning the Meeting

- Start the meeting on time.
- State the purpose of the meeting.
- Explain the agenda.

Running the Meeting

- Stick as near the time line you have prepared as you can.
- Stick to the agenda. Some straying is OK and may even be beneficial to the meeting's purpose. But, if there is too much discussion that is not on the agenda, it will be nearly impossible to cover the agenda in the time given.
- Listen. Practice some of your listening skills that you studied previously or review the application that includes some material on listening.
- Be courteous and kind to all. Politely remind others to be courteous if they are not treating others with respect.
- Make sure all meeting participants have input into the conversation. They are there for a reason and should feel encouraged to participate.

Ending the Meeting

- Explain what actions will be taken as a result of the meeting and who will take care of completing these actions.
- Tell what follow-up plans are needed.
- Announce the date, time, and place of next meeting, if applicable.
- Thank everyone for his or her contribution.

Some Common Problems in Meetings

- Poor planning
- No goal or agenda
- Straying from the subject or agenda
- Ineffective leadership
- Rambling, redundant, digressive discussions
- Dominating the discussions by certain individuals
- Disorganization and interruptions
- Not starting on time; taking too long; not ending in time allotted

4. **Recording the Minutes.** The minutes become the official record of the meeting and the actions taken in those meetings. Minutes are characterized by a clear, concise presentation of factual information, properly arranged in an acceptable format. Since minutes are frequently used for reference, every detail included in them should be complete and accurate. As a general rule, the minutes are edited for omissions and corrections by the chair or the recording secretary before they are distributed to the members. Minutes commonly include the following:

- Record of the time, date, and place of meeting
- Indicate the presiding officer (i.e., the person in charge)
- List the members present
- List the members absent
- List approval or changes to previous meeting
- Record committee reports
- Record special reports
- Discuss unfinished business—business that was not completed at the last meeting
- Open the floor for new business
- Announce time, date, and place of next meeting
- Adjourn—record the time the meeting ended

In the workplace setting, there are times when employees will work together when involved in a meeting, and there are times when you may have to work alone at a meeting. Employees need to know what is expected of them and how to minimize the amount of rewriting and revising that has to be done. The key word for meetings is *preparation.*

1. Think of a recent meeting you attended. Was there an agenda? Did you receive a copy of the minutes a week or so after the meeting? See if you can prepare, by memory, an agenda for a recent meeting you attended (a university lecture is applicable). If you have trouble constructing an agenda, perhaps the meeting was not very well organized. How could it have been better organized?

2. Take turns in your team taking minutes of group discussions. Use the method described in the memo and type the notes and present them to your team after the discussion. Team members should inform you of any updates or changes that need to be made. Once the minutes are finalized, hand them in to your CEO.

3. In the preparation of your minutes, check to see that your minutes do not contain any gender bias and that they do not, in any way, offend someone from another culture. Be careful of idioms or other language that may not be clear.

4. The memo gives some guidelines for running meetings, but does say that they are not the only guidelines. Surf the Internet to find additional guidelines. Write a short memo to Caroline, summarizing what you found and suggesting additions to the guidelines she presented to you.

5. Write a memo inviting Caroline to an upcoming meeting for all of those members who belong to the United Fund Committee. The United Fund Committee is a group of employees of GEI who solicit funds from management and employees. These funds are used to support various charities and social programs in the Mt. Pleasant area. Generally, funds are solicited once a year, in September. Prepare an agenda of items you might include in such a meeting so that when September rolls around, you will be ready for the big push for solicitation of funds.

6. Use the Internet to find the minutes of at least five meetings. Try to find minutes from various types of meetings. Note the different styles of recording minutes. Submit these minutes to the CEO with a short memo that describes each.

Example 31.1   Sample copy of minutes of a meeting.

Minutes of Facilities Planning Committee Meeting
Regular Monthly Meeting, April 5, 200-

Time/Date/Place	10:30 a.m., September 1, 200-, Conference Room B
Presiding Officer	Rhonda Klickstein, Human Resources Department
Recorder	Alfredo Guama, Human Resources Department
Members Present	Aaron Berg, Constance Constanza, David Derr, Christ Everett, Alfredo Guama, Holly Jacobson, Lucinda Juarez, Jensen Wong
Members Absent	Roberto Clupka, Denise Davenport, Erik Zdeb
Minutes Approved	Minutes of the March 15, 200-, meeting were approved as distributed.
Committee Reports	Plant Expansions: Christ Everett reported that expansion of the plants in Albuquerque and Albany are proceeding as planned. Production schedules have slowed slightly during this building program, but all orders have been filled on schedule. The expansion should be completed early next year. Technology Upgrade: Holly Jacobson presented proposals from two Internet Service providers, LETSLINK, and LINKLESS. After reviewing the proposals, the committee voted to accept LETSLINK and authorized Holly Jacobson to sign the contract with that company.
Special Report	Constance Constanza presented a proposal from C. D. Rogers Outdoor Furniture Wholesalers to supply GEI with outdoor furniture for the next five years. Constanza was directed to tell C. D. Rogers to present a written, detailed report at the next meeting.
Unfinished Business	None
New Business	Study of proposal from C. D. Rogers Outdoor Furniture Wholesalers at next meeting.
Adjournment	The meeting was adjourned at 12:15 p.m.

Respectfully submitted

Alfredo Guama, Recorder

Cover Letters

Susan Thomas knew it was time to ask all employees for the yearly update of their resumes. It is GEI's policy to do this so that they have an up-to-date record of the skills and qualifications of their employees when considering them for transfer or promotion. This year, she thought to herself, I'm going to ask them to include a cover letter with their resume in which they can mention any special skills I should note. Today's memo will help you to write that cover letter. Susan also supplied a sample cover letter (see Example 32.1) for your reference.

GEI

12345 GEI Place	Mt. Pleasant, Michigan 48859	517.555.1000

TO: All Employees

FROM: Susan Thomas, VP Human Resources

DATE: December 8, 200-

SUBJECT: Cover Letters

Cover letters are as important in the job search as your resume. The custom cover letter supplies the personal touch and individuality needed in a job campaign. The resume talks only about you. The cover letter deals with the specific areas in which you can benefit the needs of GEI, or any other employer. An effective letter should motivate the person reading it to review your resume and ideally invite you for an interview. It can turn your resume message into an individualized communication. Customize each letter for each organization to which you send it.

An effective cover letter enhances your resume's chances of getting attention by stressing your most relevant accomplishments and skills. A cover letter shows how you can fill the particular needs of a position in a unique way. It also gives the senior staff at GEI, or any employer, an idea of how you organize your thoughts and communicate in the written word.

Personalize each cover letter by addressing it to a specific individual in the Human Resources Department or the person with the hiring authority, using his or her full name and correct title. At GEI, you can address it either to Ms. Susan Thomas in Human Resources, or to Mr. Larry Switzer, CEO. When someone does not have the name of a person, he or she should call the company and ask for the name and title of the head of Human Resources (spelled correctly!).

In a cover letter, as in your resume, don't get too personal and don't give too much information—save most of it for the interview. Normally, your salary requirement is not given in a cover letter, but be ready to discuss it in an interview.

A cover letter is usually three or four paragraphs long and covers one page. The first paragraph tells the reader why you are writing and why you are interested in the company and the position.

The second paragraph refers to the accomplishments on your resume that relate to the contribution you can make to GEI, or any company. Mention that it appears that your skills are very compatible with the qualifications the company is seeking. While you do not want to restate exactly what is on your resume, which will be attached with the letter, you do want to relate your experiences to their needs. Your goal here is to make a connection between your skills and the requirements of the position for which you are applying.

In the final paragraph, make a direct request for an interview. State when you will be available and say that you will follow up with a telephone call to request a mutually convenient time for an interview. Thank the person for his or her consideration.

When you are answering an advertisement from a newspaper, carefully read the ad and pretend you wrote it. Think of what response you would look for if you were the employment interviewer. Again, use specific references to how you fit the specific requirements outlined in the ad. Tailor your response to each ad.

Important Warnings!

1. No life stories—no one has the time (or interest!) to read all about you.
2. *Never* send a form letter—customize each letter.
3. No typographical, grammatical, or spelling errors in your letter (or resume).
4. Do not include anything irrelevant—if it does not contribute to your getting an interview, don't include it.

A carefully written cover letter calls attention to your special qualities, which will help get you an interview.

1. Write a cover letter, with an attached resume, for the following position. You may make any reasonable assumptions necessary to fit your qualifications with the specifications of the ad.

PRODUCTION SUPERVISOR

Because of national expansion, Goodtimes Enterprises, Inc., has immediate openings for **PRODUCTION SUPERVISORS** in their Dallas, TX, plant. Candidates should have a minimum of 2 years supervisory experience in a manufacturing environment. The ideal candidate will possess strong employee relations skills, including the ability to train, motivate, and develop employees. Must also possess strong communication skills.
Please send resume with cover letter to:
Ms. Susan Thomas, Vice President, Human Resources
Goodtimes Enterprises, Inc.
12345 Oak Boulevard, Mt. Pleasant, MI 48858

diversity

2. Write a cover letter, with an attached resume, for the following position. You may make any reasonable assumptions necessary to meet the specifications of the advertisement. It may be helpful to review Application 4 before beginning this assignment.

Human Resource Generalist Wanted!

Goodtimes Enterprises, Inc., is expanding internationally and has an excellent opportunity for an HR Generalist with hands-on experience in employee relations. The right person also will be familiar with global recruiting, intercultural training programs, and benefits administration. This highly visible position requires a college degree, excellent oral/written communication skills, and the ability to work with all levels of management. Please forward your resume and cover letter to:
Mr. Karl Schmidt, Vice President, Human Resources
Goodtimes Enterprises, Inc., Weinstadt Subsidiary
Bahnhofstr, 13, 6000
Weinstadt 2 GERMANY

ethics

3. A friend of yours has answered an ad for what she considers to be her "dream" job. The ad states that anyone applying for the position must have a minimum cumulative grade point average of 3.0. Your friend's grade point average is 2.6. She more than meets all other requirements for the job. Fearing that she won't get an interview if she tells the truth, in her cover letter she states that she meets the company's grade point requirement. Discuss this decision with your team members for a few minutes. Your CEO will pick one person from each team to sit on a panel and lead a class discussion on the issue. Please include possible future effects on her career if her "little white lie" is discovered.

Example 32.1   Sample cover letter.

December 10, 200-

Ms. Susan Thomas
Vice President of Human Resources
Goodtimes Enterprises, Inc.
12345 Oak Boulevard
Mt. Pleasant, MI 48859

Dear Ms. Thomas:

Thank you for taking time from your busy schedule yesterday to discuss the possibilities of joining the Management Training Program at Goodtimes Enterprises, Inc. At your request, my resume is attached. This letter outlines some of the experiences mentioned during our telephone discussion and cited on my resume that have prepared me well for successfully completing your training program.

As demonstrated on my resume, I have gained valuable experience in sales techniques and customer relations through my position at Lechmere's. I have learned the importance of meeting the customer's needs and financial capabilities. These skills have been very successful for me, resulting in my being named Outstanding Salesman of the Month several times for meeting or exceeding sales quotas. My experience as a disc jockey at a local radio station where I organized and broadcast a successful three-hour weekly show for four years provided an excellent opportunity to hone my communication skills.

In addition to my work experience, my educational background has prepared me for a management trainee position. I have completed coursework in marketing management, marketing research, operations management, human resource management, and international trade. Additional courses in marketing and management have complemented my management major.

I am eager to discuss the opportunity of applying my talents and experience to the Management Training Program at Goodtimes Enterprises, Inc. As you suggested, I will call next week regarding the status of my application and to make arrangements for a mutually convenient meeting time. Thank you for your consideration.

Sincerely,

Anthony Parrinello

Enclosure

Resumes

GEI believes in promoting from within the company whenever possible. Susan Thomas, therefore, is asking every employee at GEI to submit a resume and cover letter (see Application 32) to the Human Resources Department to keep on file. Those employees whose qualifications best fit openings within the company will be given an opportunity for promotion or to be transferred to one of GEI's subsidiaries. She has sent all employees the following memo which explains the format that GEI asks employees to use when writing their resumes, and an example of a resume (see Example 33.1) for you to refer to.

| 12345 GEI Place | Mt. Pleasant, Michigan 48859 | 517.555.1000 |

TO: All Employees

FROM: Susan Thomas, VP Human Resources

DATE: December 13, 200-

SUBJECT: Writing a Resume

A resume is a selling document. With it you will be selling the most valuable product you will ever sell—yourself! A resume is a printed synopsis of your educational and work experiences and accomplishments. It is *not* a novel; it is a capsule biography, which communicates the maximum amount of relevant information about you through a minimum number of words. For your resume (you) to be considered, it must hit home immediately. It has been estimated that the average resume has about 45 seconds to make an impression, either positive or negative, during this initial screening.

Your resume should be 100 percent honest. Falsification of facts is certain to be harmful, and can be cause for immediate dismissal from GEI, or any company, if it learns that there is false or misleading information on a resume. Avoid putting information in a resume that would cause your resume (you) to be screened out. Stress your assets rather than your liabilities. GEI, and most employers, prefer a short, concise resume of one to two pages. One page is usually sufficient for most college graduates with limited work experience.

What Should Be Included in a Resume?

The first rule of resume writing is that there are no hard and fast rules. An effective resume will reflect your "uniqueness" as an individual. The factual information to be included in your resume(s) will be dependent on your background and experiences as well as the position(s) you seek. The resume must be uniquely yours. GEI does ask employees to include several of the following basic categories of data in their resumes, dictated not by theory or fad, but by common sense and business ethics.

1. **Name, Address, Telephone Number.** Your name generally appears in capital letters at the top center of the page. Your address should be next. It is where you can most frequently be contacted by mail and/or telephone. For most people this would be their home address; however, personal circumstances may influence your decision. You may wish to include a college or university address and telephone number.

2. **Employment Objective.** A well-written objective demonstrates goal orientation, focus, and a degree of career planning that is viewed favorably by employers. It gives your resume a definite vision. It should appear at the beginning of the first page immediately after your name, address, and telephone number. State the position you desire in concise terms. Do not include more than one objective, or a widely diversified objective in the same resume. Diligent employment-seekers will tailor a separate resume to each job for which they apply.

   If you do not know what you want to do, it's hard to formulate a career objective. The most common error made by resume writers is that their objective is not specific. An effective resume is designed with a specific employment objective or position in mind. This is commonly referred to as resume focus. Once your objective is established, check to make sure that information included on your resume matches your employment objective. In other words, if your employment objective is to become a marketing manager, include and highlight all data that would relate to that type of position.

3. **Education.** Educational background and special training go in this section. The sequence in which the categories Education and Work Experience are included in a resume depend on individual preference. The education category of a recent college graduate with little work experience will be more important than that of a 40-year-old whose work experience will make up the bulk of the resume. Thus, the new graduate may choose to put his or her education before work experience. For the employment-seeker with extensive work experience, the education category may include only those institutions from which the degrees were received along with graduation dates. A brief statement of any academic honors or scholarships (e.g., Dean's List, etc.) may go here, or you may wish to have a special section entitled, "Honors and Activities." These are personal choices. Team members who have a high GPA may wish to include it in this section.

4. **Work Experience.** This category is the most important section of your resume. GEI, and other employers, hire with specific company needs in mind. Once again, take the employer's point of view. Your work experiences should highlight what you have done and what you can offer the employer.

   When preparing this category, your first step might be to evaluate the extent and relevancy of your work experiences. A careful evaluation will enable you to make decisions about the manner in which you organize this category as well as the content you will include. Place your work experiences in reverse chronological order. Let your summer or part-time experience follow the full-time positions.

   Remember that your work experiences are unique to you; therefore, the work experience category should reflect that uniqueness.

If your work experience is minimal, an internship, cooperative education programs, student teaching, laboratory assistantships, or a research project should be listed first in this category, especially if they relate to the position you seek.

5. **Personal Data/Honors and Activities/Outside Activities.** Whatever you decide to name this category, remember that GEI, and all employers, are interested in hiring, promoting, and transferring people who have been, or presently are, active in a variety of academic, extracurricular, or social activities either on campus or in the community. It indicates that you are motivated and get involved, obviously very positive work traits. You should attempt to view yourself through the eyes of an employer. This category is usually placed near the end of the resume. This gives the employer the opportunity to consider relevant, job-related information prior to considering your personal data.

6. **Other Categories.** You may elect to include your own special categories. Please do so if you feel the information is relevant. Be creative and use your imagination.

Warnings!

Your resume is a reflection of you, and what you put in it is your choice, but there are pitfalls to avoid. You want it to represent you in the best possible way.

1. **Too Long.** One page is preferred especially for undergraduates; use two pages only if you have substantial experience.

2. **Poorly Organized.** There should be a logical order to your resume. Pick one format and stick to it. If the arrangement of your resume is not constant, it will be hard to follow and difficult to read.

3. **Poorly Keyboarded or Printed.** There should be no typographical, spelling, or grammatical errors on your resume. Be sure your printer is working perfectly. If possible, use a laser printer with easy to read fonts. You are striving for a professional appearance.

4. **Poorly Written.** Poor grammar or poor sentence construction can be reasons you don't get an interview. Don't overuse the same adjectives (how many times have you used the word "challenge"?). Be concise rather than wordy.

5. **Poor Career Objective.** An objective should not be too long or too short. It must be clearly defined and tailored to each job for which you apply.

6. **Poor Description of Experience.** Be specific and action oriented in the description of your various work experiences.

7. **Irrelevant Personal Information.** Height, weight, marital status, gender, age, number of dependents, religion, race, national origin, and the like are not job related. Leave them out of your resume.

8. **Overdone.** Fancy typesetting and binders, photographs, and exotic paper stock are generally not appropriate for the business world. You are usually better off using 25 percent bond off white paper.

9. **Poorly Presented.** Many resumes arrive in the Human Resources Department with no apparent connections to the organization or a specific job. A well-tailored cover letter helps to customize your resume (see Application 32).

10. **Too Boastful.** If the resume does not honestly reflect job duties and accomplishments, or the truth is stretched too far, it will come out in an interview or during a reference check. Be 100 percent honest.

A resume is always a work in progress. It will be utilized continually throughout your work life to provide information about you when you are being considered for a promotion or for an employment search.

1. Prepare two resumes—one to apply for a transfer to one of the national divisions that GEI is building, and one for an international site. How do they differ? *Note:* It will be helpful to review Application 4 for this assignment.

2. Bring your resumes to class on a day your CEO designates. Exchange resumes with other team members, so that everyone has a resume other than their own. Critique the resume that you have. After a few minutes, form a circle with your team members and one-by-one, discuss the resume that you have with the group. Tell them the points that you like about it, and, if there are any suggestions you have for improving it, state them diplomatically.

Example 33.1   Sample resume.

SARAH GRACE PERROTT

Present Address   Permanent Address:
Siena College, SPOB 1016   9 Craiwell Avenue
515 Loudon Road   Westfield, MA 01085
Loudonville, NY 12211   (413) 555-0710
(518) 555-4274; E-mail: SGP4405@Siena.EDU

OBJECTIVE: A position in marketing management with specific interest in brand management and advertising.

EDUCATION: Siena College
Loudonville, NY 12211
B.S. in Marketing, May 2000
GPA: 3.7
International Study, Spring, 1999
Regents College, London, England

COMPUTER   WordPerfect, MICROSOFT Word and Excel97, PowerPoint, Windows98,
SKILLS: Netscape

HONORS: Siena College Presidential Scholar
Honors Student, four years
Elected to the Siena College 21st Century Leaders Society, Class of 2000
Chosen to participate in selection of Residence Life Staff for 1998–1999

EXPERIENCE: **Public Relations Intern**   Summers 1998–99
American Management Association, New York, NY
Promoted newly published books through descriptive press releases targeted
toward critics, magazines, and newspapers. Coordinated and booked regional
tours with television and radio stations for authors. Recorded and processed
orders for bookstores nationwide.

Admissions Office Intern   September 1999–May 2000
Siena College, Loudonville, NY
Revised and adapted media guides and brochures to promote the college to
prospective students. Researched and prepared articles on college activities
and events. Compiled and distributed weekly press releases. Arranged interviews with media when appropriate.

Resident Assistant   August 1997–May 1999
Siena College, Loudonville,NY
Organized, planned, and implemented various programs within a residence
hall of 250 students. Served as a liaison between administration and residents.
Counseled students with personal, academic, and extracurricular concerns.

Personnel Assistant   May 1999–August 1999
Town of Westfield, Westfield, MA
General assistant to Personnel Clerk and Employee Benefits Clerk. Established
personnel files for new employees and updated existing files. Coordinated
Worker's Compensation cases. Notified employees of benefit changes and
pending company events.

ACTIVITIES: Photography Club (four years); Siena Admissions Tour Guide; Campus Min-
istry Greeter; Sophomore Advisory Committee; Hall Council Representative;
Speakers Committee; Management Leadership Club.

Interviewing

Susan Thomas was finished reviewing all of the employee resumes and cover letters that GEI employees had submitted to update their files. Many employees had also expressed interest in transferring to other GEI sites and/or for promotions to positions that were open. Larry Switzer had asked her to present him with a slate of employees he could interview for some of the available positions. Today's memo will help you plan for the interview process.

| 12345 GEI Place | Mt. Pleasant, Michigan 48859 | 517.555.1000 |

TO:	All Employees
FROM:	Susan Thomas, VP Human Resources
DATE:	December 18, 200-
SUBJECT:	Interviewing

An interview provides the opportunity to persuade an interviewer that you are the best candidate for a particular position. Careful preparation and effective communication have a strong influence on the outcome of the interview.

Prior to an interview, review your goals and values. Know not only *what* you want, but *why* you want it. Your ability to market yourself well is in direct proportion to your level of preparation. Ask for a copy of the job description prior to the interview, if possible. Read the position description carefully, so you can explain exactly how your qualifications meet the specifications for the job. Be prepared to state in specific terms why you want this particular job.

Research the company. One of the biggest confidence builders for a job interview is to have a thorough knowledge of the organization. Learn about its services/products, clients, size, organization structure, including subsidiaries, its products and profitability, its competitors, position in the market, potential new markets, and projections for the future of the organization and the industry. Review its Web page.

The only way to learn how to interview is to *practice, practice, PRACTICE.* For many people, talking about themselves is a difficult task, so be prepared to respond to such questions as "Tell me about yourself" and "Why should I select you?" Practice your responses either alone or in mock interviews with friends. This will increase your confidence.

An interviewer is trying to determine whether you are the best candidate for the position. He or she must make a judgment about you as a complete package. He or she is looking at you as a probable employee based on a number of factors called *predictors of success:*

Personal Impressions. A good first impression is important. From the beginning of the interview you will be evaluated on such personal traits as personal appearance, poise, ability to communicate, maturity, stability, integrity, self-reliance.

Job Qualifications. Your basic qualifications for the job are, of course, of great importance. No matter how well you have defined and demonstrated what you want to do, which cannot be underestimated, the final decision regarding an offer of employment primarily will be made based on your academic and work qualifications.

Your Obligations

Your ability to answer questions in a sincere, positive, and organized manner will demonstrate your preparation for the interview. Your objective is to make the interview a shared conversation. It should not be an interrogation. There are also a few behavior guidelines that can add to its success.

Arrival. Be punctual. Arrive 10 to 15 minutes before the interview. If you cannot make the appointment, call well in advance to cancel or reschedule.

Establish Rapport. Greet the interviewer by name, smile and give a firm handshake. Maintain eye contact, and be aware of your other nonverbal behavior. Your tone of voice, posture, facial expression, and eye contact all give clues about your feelings and attitudes. Don't fidget or slouch. Face the interviewer in a relaxed, open manner. Give the interviewer a chance to find out that you are a genuine, capable, and sincere individual. Be friendly, warm, and enthusiastic. Employers hire people they like and who appear genuinely interested in the position.

Communication. Your answers should be clear and to the point. Avoid one-word responses as well as long, rambling explanations. Your communication skills include being able to introduce a point, elaborate on it and close. Remember—you will only have about 30 minutes to sell yourself! Speak clearly and directly. Don't interrupt. Use all your active listening skills. This is a vital part of communicating. Ask for clarification if you don't understand a point the interviewer makes. Above all, avoid using fillers such as *um-m-m, ah-h-h, like,* and *you know.*

Getting Your Message Across. Be prepared to define your career goals and how your skills and achievements meet the position requirements. Talk about ways you can contribute to the company. Emphasize your strengths, but be prepared to talk about your weaknesses if asked. Focus on skills or personal qualities that would be beneficial to the organization. Give examples from jobs, internships and other educational experiences, extracurricular or volunteer activities, and personal interests to support this. Express a willingness to learn and ability to work hard.

Summarize. Reiterate briefly why you should be hired. Thank the interviewer for his or her time and interest. Tell him or her that you would like to be considered further for the position and that you look forward to another interview. Reinforce that you are very interested in the position and that you hope for a favorable decision.

Interview Format

All interviews follow the basic communication guideline of having a beginning, a middle, and an end. Most screening interviews involve the following stages:

Introduction. The interviewer "breaks the ice" and establishes a positive atmosphere. While this appears to be a simple conversation between two strangers, first impressions are being made and are critical in the decision-making process. The interviewer begins forming his or her opinions from the opening seconds of the interview. Your initial comments, general appearance, voice, manner, energy, and enthusiasm will significantly contribute to his or her overall impression.

Exploration of Your Background. During the second stage, the interviewer asks questions concerning education, work experience, activities, and interests. You may be asked to describe how you have set and achieved goals, handled difficult situations, analyzed and resolved problems, or persuaded others to take actions you have defined. This is when careful preparation pays off. Be sure to respond to questions in enough detail to provide a full understanding of the experience being described, but try to keep responses concise. Avoid any extreme modesty or boastfulness. Try to provide the interviewer with concrete statements and examples that support claims regarding ability or potential.

Employer Information. You should be able to enter into a dialogue concerning how you can benefit the company. Now is the time to ask intelligent, probing questions that give you more in-depth information about the company's needs. Well-constructed questions show interest and competence. Information provided will help you to fully understand the nature of the position and to decide whether you want the position.

Conclusion. The interviewer will usually provide some indication that the interview is drawing to a close. You will be given an opportunity to make final remarks and ask final questions. Thank the interviewer for the opportunity to discuss the position in which you are interested.

Important Warnings

There are some behaviors and actions that can have a negative effect on an interview. They can lead to your being rejected for further consideration.

1. Lack of planning for the interview
2 No definite career goals
3. Poor personal appearance
4. Lack of enthusiasm about the company or position
5. Lack of social skills
6. Poor eye contact
7. Limp handshake
8. Vague responses to questions
9. Poor vocabulary, grammar, or diction
10. Overemphasis on salary, for example, expecting too much too soon

Remember, the interview is your opportunity *to make something happen*. It is your responsibility to sell yourself so that an employment decision will be made in your favor.

1. With your project team, prepare a list of questions you would ask if you were an interviewer. When you have finished, compare lists among project teams. How many similar questions appear on each list? Compile a master list of questions, some of which can be used in the next item.

2. Interview role play. Your CEO will distribute some of the resumes and cover letters you have completed to each work team for review. From the resumes, each team will select one person to be interviewed for the position in Texas and one for the position in Weinstadt, Germany. The project manager of each team will interview the candidates for the national position and the CEO will interview the candidate for the international position. Your CEO will give you further instructions.

3. A friend of yours has applied for a position at GEI. She has completed the interview process, and has given your name as a reference. You know this person uses illegal substances and often drinks too much alcohol. In fact, you know the reason she had to leave her last job was that she was caught using an illegal substance on the job. You feel sorry for her, so you decide you will give her a good recommendation and not say anything about her substance abuse problem. Discuss the ethical issues associated with this decision with your project team, and then write a collaborative memo to your CEO, explaining your team's position on the issue.

Employment Letters

Whe hen you saw Susan Thomas at lunch earlier today, she said she had something to talk with you about. "I'll send you a memo after lunch that should explain what I want you to do." You are thrilled to be able to complete another task for Susan.

| 12345 GEI Place | Mt. Pleasant, Michigan 48859 | 517.555.1000 |

TO: Project Director

FROM: Susan Thomas, VP Human Resources

DATE: April 29, 200-

SUBJECT: Employment Letters

Alfreda Gonza, business teacher at the local high school, sent me a memo last week asking whether or not GEI has a set of employment letters that we could give her to distribute to her students.

Alfreda teaches a two-week unit on writing application letters and resumes. However, she has very little material on other kinds of employment letters. She is thinking specifically of such letters as the following:

- A job-inquiry letter
- An application follow-up letter
- A job-acceptance letter
- A job-refusal letter
- Thank-you letter following the interview

I think she has a good idea. These kinds of materials would be very helpful for students to have in their job search.

Can you come up with a series of guidelines and/or samples of each of these kinds of letters so that I can send a copy to Alfreda that she can duplicate and give to her students.

You have always done well with any project I have given you, and I think this one will be no exception. Good luck. I'll expect the project in my office within two weeks.

Guidelines for Preparing Employment Letters

Job-Inquiry Letter (see Example 35.1)

- Write a job-inquiry letter to a company in which you are interested even though they have not posted a job opening.
- Keep the letter short.
- Give the reasons you are writing (e.g., moving to the area, finishing a college degree, working in a company that can use your qualifications, living in an area that is satisfying to you, etc.).
- Use plain paper with your return address neatly typed. If you are currently working for a company, do not use letterhead paper from that company.
- Proofread the letter carefully and correct all errors.

Application Follow-Up Letter (see Example 35.2)

- Write an application follow-up letter if you have not heard from your initial application.
- Keep the letter short.
- Remind the reader that you want your original application in the active file.
- Tell the reader what else you have done since you sent in your original application (e.g., enrolled in another course at the local community college, completed the internship in accounting, did some part-time accounting work on a consulting basis for a local company, etc.).
- Use plain paper with your return address neatly typed.
- Proofread the letter carefully and correct all errors.

A Job-Acceptance Letter (see Example 35.3)

- Use the deductive-style of writing (the acceptance goes in the first paragraph).
- Return any security forms, health records, or other papers you have been asked to complete.
- Keep the letter short.
- Use plain paper with your return address neatly typed.
- Proofread the letter carefully and correct all errors.

Job-Refusal Letter (see Example 35.4)

- Use the inductive-style letter. Lead in to the fact that you cannot accept the job for the reasons stated.
- Thank the reader for offering the job.

- Keep the letter short.
- Proofread the letter carefully and correct all errors.

Thank-You Letter Following an Interview (see Example 35.5)

- Write a thank-you letter to all persons who were involved in your interview. Thank them for all the courtesies they have shown you.
- Keep the thank-you letter short and to the point.
- Say that you will follow any suggestions that the interviewers have given to you (e.g., enroll in an additional computer course, take a course in cost accounting, get more work experience, complete an internship, etc.).
- Use plain paper with your return address neatly typed.
- Proofread the letter carefully and correct all errors.

Job Responsibilities

1. Use the sample letters that follow and prepare one of each of the letters. Use information that applies to you. Do not copy the letters word for word. Use the samples to generate ideas for your own set of letters.

2. Discuss with your team what other employment situations exist for which you could prepare a letter to have available as a model.

3. Do an Internet search to see if you can find more information about employment letters. Prepare a short memo to your boss, with a copy to Alfreda Gonza. Alert Alfreda to the fact that she can find additional information on the Internet. Include the Web site within the memo.

4. In your team setting, check all letters written by members of your team to see if all letters are free from bias and prejudice.

5. Check all team letters to see if there are any violations of ethics. Are letters honest, truthful, and correct? Discuss.

Example 35.1   Sample job-inquiry letter.

12345 East Main Street
Mt. Pleasant, MI 48859
April 30, 200-

Ms. Brunhilda Vundtka
Human Resources/Personnel
The Pennington Group
98748 West Eight Mile Road
Detroit, MI 45876

Dear Ms. Vundtka:

May I please have an application form for work in your actuarial department? I am finishing my college degree, which includes several courses in mathematics, statistics, and accounting information systems.

My husband and I plan to make our home in the Detroit area after I graduate on May 15.

Sincerely,

Your Name

Example 35.2   Sample application follow-up.

12345 East Main Street
Mt. Pleasant, MI 48859
May 1, 200-

Mr. Adolph Gutmann, Manager
The Gutmann Industries
9876 North Punxsutawney Street
Philadelphia, PA 39875

Dear Mr. Gutmann:

Since I wrote to you about an accounting position with your company, I have completed three additional courses in accounting, one additional course in accounting information systems, and a business communications course.

Please do keep my application in the active file and let me know when you need to add another accountant.

Sincerely,

Your Name

Example 35.3   Sample job-acceptance letter.

12345 East Main Street
Mt. Pleasant, MI 48859
May 5, 200-

Ms. Roberta MacEntire
Director of Marketing Research
Marketco Corporation
56748 Northern Lights Boulevard
Anchorage, AL 98746

Dear Ms. MacEntire:

Yes! I accept your offer of a job in the Marketing Research Division at Marketco.

Here are the security clearance forms you provided me. Also enclosed are the health forms you need, a copy of my birth certificate, and all of the other information that is asked for on the form you gave me.

Thank you for introducing me to many of the marketing people in your firm. I know that I will enjoy working with all of you.

Sincerely,

Your Name
Enclosure

Example 35.4   Sample job-refusal letter.

12345 East Main Street
Mt. Pleasant, MI 48859
May 15, 200-

Ms. Consuella Schultz, Director
Personnel Planning
Fire & Ice Corporation
Pataskala, OH 45675

Dear Ms. Schultz:

Yours was one of the most interesting job interviews I had in my search for a position in sales and marketing research. I especially remember your ideas on the various ways to spice up the research.

As you pointed out, opportunities at Fire & Ice are exceedingly good. Your promotion plan and your bonus incentive plan were both very well outlined and planned. But since my major interest in sales is limited to wholesalers, I have taken a job with Miller Magic Mops, where my responsibilities will be working with wholesalers only.

Thank you so much for the time you spent with me.

Sincerely,

Your Name

Example 35.5   Sample thank-you letter following an interview.

12345 East Main Street
Mt. Pleasant, MI 48859
May 20, 200-

Ms. Audra Tucken
Human Resources Department
The WXYZ Corporation
Grand Forks, ND 58201

Dear Ms. Tucken:

Thank you for taking the time to interview me last Monday. You made me feel very welcome.

At your suggestion, I have enrolled in a two-week class of PowerPoint presentations at the local community college. After I complete the course, I will call you for the second interview, as you suggested.

I look forward to seeing you again soon.

Sincerely,

Your Name

Finding a Job

Job opportunities are everywhere and for everybody. Today, millions of people in the United States hold a job. Employers are constantly looking for workers to fill job vacancies because of retirements, resignations, transfers, or promotions. When you talk with Susan Thomas this morning at the coffee break, she tells you that she has another request from the high school business teacher, Alfreda Gonza. Alfreda really liked the material you prepared for her students on employment follow-up letters. "Now, she has another request," Susan says. "I'll send you a memo this afternoon explaining her latest request." She does.

12345 GEI Place	Mt. Pleasant, Michigan 48859	517.555.1000

TO:	Project Directors
FROM:	Susan Thomas, VP Human Resources
DATE:	May 1, 200-
SUBJECT:	Alfreda Gonza's Request

Alfreda Gonza called me this morning with another request. As I mentioned to you earlier today, she was thrilled with the material we sent her about employment follow-up letters. Now she has a new request, and I think you are just the person to prepare the materials.

Alfreda wants some material for her students on how to go about considering job offers. How should students begin the job search? Where should they begin? How do they find leads for job offers? I think these are legitimate questions and that we should be able to send her some information.

What do you think? Can you do it?

So, you begin to prepare the information for Alfreda. You will spend a little time on the project. For your basic outline, you prepare the following material:

How to Get a Job

Finding a job is in itself a full-time job. Only the persistent survive. You must plan your job search thoroughly and efficiently. Here are some principles I came up with that might help you. Also, a list of assignments is attached that will help you understand the list of principles.

Before you begin be sure you do the following:

- Analyze your career goals. What do you want to do? What are your plans for your life? What kinds of jobs do you need to reach your life's employment goal? What kind of job will make you happy?

- Analyze your skills and abilities. Do you have the kind of education and training that the job you are seeking requires? Or are you aiming for a position that exceeds your skills? Are you interested in the job itself or only in the salary it pays?

- Find out the job opportunities in your chosen field. Are there a lot of jobs in this field? Or are the jobs limited? Will the job require you to change locations? Are you willing to move to another state or another country if required to do so?

- Be sure your credentials are in order. Do you have a top-notch resume? Will the resume itself demand that people read it? Is the resume error free? Do you know how to write a letter of application? Do you know how to prepare follow-up employment communications?

- Search for possible job vacancies. How do you know a vacancy exists? How can you find out if a certain company has a vacancy?

The following list of "to-do's" will be good sources to help you find out about job vacancies:

- Visit your educational placement office. Any schools you have attended usually have trained individuals who specialize in the area of employment. In high school, you should talk to your vocational guidance counselor. In college, visit the career placement office.

- Get leads from friends, relatives, neighbors, teachers, and acquaintances. Your parents will probably know much more about the community and what organizations may be hiring.

- Read the help-wanted advertisements. While you are in school, your first job may be a part-time one. The best way to use the help-wanted ads is to read and study them carefully. Determine which ads you want to pursue based on your qualifications, your training, and your experience.

- Visit all types of employment offices. Business firms are always searching for employees. So are government bureaus, local, state, and national. Look in the local telephone directory to find these sources. Match your abilities with those of the organization.

- Consider all possibilities. Don't overlook the small companies. Many times, when one is looking for a job, he or she considers only large corporations. You may find that smaller businesses have a lot to offer; for instance, small department stores, specialty shops, banks, hospitals, grocery stores.

- Let people know that you are looking for a job and that you want a job. You may even wish to advertise in the local newspaper under "Situations Wanted." Tell all of your friends you're job hunting.

- Be your own boss. Many ideas for self-employment exist; there are, for example, such things as becoming a salesperson, opening a bakery (if you can bake), opening a candy store (if you can make candy), opening an office supply store, and lots of others. You will need start-up cash, business plans, and lots of assistance.

Job Responsibilities

teamwork

1. As a team, prepare a list of places where you might find posted notices for job openings. Discuss your findings with all of the employees.

2. Name one or more individuals at your school, along with their office location, who can help you with job opportunities.

3. List five friends from whom you might obtain information about a job opening. List five relatives who may help you. List five others who may help you. Give names, addresses, and phone numbers where you can contact these individuals.

diversity

4. Search the help-wanted columns and find an advertisement describing the type of job in which you are interested. Bring the advertisements to class. Are any ethics violated in the ad? Is the ad clearly free of bias and prejudices? Discuss.

technology

5. Search the Internet for types of jobs in which you are interested. Prepare a list of companies where you might work at this job. Discuss the list with the other employees.

6. List five government agencies (local, state, national) that may be in need of your abilities.

7. List five small businesses in your area where your skills might be put to use.

8. Compose a job advertisement for the local newspaper describing your abilities.

9. List five persons in your neighborhood who have been successful in self-employment. Investigate "why" they have been so successful. Compile your findings for class discussion.

Appendix

Selected Style Techniques of Writing

Emphasizing Clarity in Writing

1. Vary the structure and the length of sentences. When you wish to illustrate "power" in your writing, use a short, simple sentence.

2. Use "action" verbs to achieve an active voice in your writing. Use "passive" verbs sparingly, as this results in a passive voice. In an active voice, the subject of the sentence *acts*. In a passive voice, the subject of the sentence is *acted upon*.

   a. Elmo Plotkins *prepared* the plans for the new music hall. (Subject of the sentence—Elmo Plotkins—acts—*active voice*.)

   b. The *plans* for the new music hall were prepared by Elmo Plotkins. (Subject of the sentence—plans—is acted upon—*passive voice*.)

3. Use short words so that your reader will understand them. Long words are sometimes not understood clearly by the reader or the writer. Sometimes a writer may be trying to show how *intelligent* he or she is.

   a. I will *endeavor* to get the report to you immediately. (*Endeavor* is too long and not as understandable as the word, *try.*)

   b. I will *try* to get the report to you immediately. Even better: I *will get* the report to you immediately.

4. Improve your vocabulary. Even though you should avoid using long, complicated words, you should know what those words mean. A good way to improve and develop your vocabulary is to spend time reading—reading novels, reports, newspapers, journals, magazines, or anything else you can get your hands on.

5. Use "picture" words—words your reader can understand and relate to. Use short, concrete words your reader can visualize.

6. Use a conversational tone. Generally, write the way you speak—and you should speak well. Avoid stuffy business jargon. Use lots of the "YOU" attitude.

7. Use variety in your sentence structure. Do not fall into the trap of the subject-verb-object sequence, unless you change the order once in a while. Use object first occasionally.

   a. He (subject) never told (verb) a bigger lie (object).

   b. A bigger lie (object) he (subject) never told (verb).

Adding Emphasis to Writing

1. Use lists to break up complex statements. Lists must be grammatically parallel in structure. Each item in a listing should begin with the same part of

speech. You may number each item, you may give each item an alphabetical character, or you may use bullets (•) for emphasis.

2. Use mechanical devices for emphasis. Many ways exist to add emphasis to your writing. Here are some of them:

   a. Special formats—use lines or boxes to set off something special

   b. All capital letters

   c. **Bolding**

   d. *Italics*

   e. A dash—within a sentence

   f. <u>Underlining</u>

   g. Color

Using Basic Sentence Patterns for Effective Communication

1. Use a *simple* sentence to show power, spreading the good news, and creating emphasis. A simple sentence contains a complete thought, sometimes called an independent clause. A simple sentence presents one idea and one idea only.

   As we were flying off to our vacation in Lake Tahoe, one of the plane's engines caught fire. The pilot told us we would have to to to go back to the airport immediately. *I was frightened.* (Power emphasis using the simple sentence)

2. Use a *compound* sentence when you want to bring about a balanced relationship in the sentence or when you want to show contrast. A compound sentence is two or more independent clauses joined by a conjunction and a comma or joined by a semicolon without a conjunction.

   We were flying off to our vacation in Lake Tahoe; one of the plane's engines caught fire. The pilot decided to return to the airport, *but* we were all frightened.

3. A *complex* sentence is used to de-emphasize a thought. A complex sentence contains at least two clauses: one independent and one or more dependent clauses. The main thought in a complex sentence should be placed in the independent clause. Use the dependent clause to deemphasize the thought.

   If you arrive before I do, please wait for me.

   Although I did not do well on the final examination, I did manage to pass the course.

4. A *compound-complex* sentence is also used to de-emphasize a thought. A compound-complex sentence contains three or more clauses—at least two independent clauses and one dependent clause. A compound-complex sentence establishes a complicated relationship.

   As all of you realize, a chance exists that the company may be downsized; and many of you may be let go.

   If you arrive before I do, please wait for me; but I may be as late as 15 minutes.

Additional Writing Hints

1. Use *explicit* (or specific) language to emphasize a point or a positive situation.

   GEI wishes you well in your new position as Project Director.

   Instead of

   GEI wishes you well in your career move.

2. Use *implicit* (or implied) language to de-emphasize a point or in a negative situation.

GEI is sorry to hear about your wife.

Instead of

GEI is sorry to hear about your wife's untimely accident leading to her violent death.

3. Use verbs, pronouns, gender, and number so that they agree with the words to which they refer.

John and Alyssa *is* going to the game tonight. (Does not agree)

John and Alyssa *are* going to the game tonight. (Agrees)

Each of us must do *their* duty. (Does not agree)

Each of must do *his or her* duty. (Agrees)

All of us must do *our* duty. (Agrees)

Alyssa left *his* book at the library. (Does not agree)

Alyssa left *her* book at the library. (Agrees)

4. Use a *noun* after a demonstrative pronoun for clarity. Demonstrative pronouns are *this, that, these,* and *those.*

This will help reduce misunderstanding. (Lacks clarity)

This **plan** will help reduce misunderstanding. (Provides clarity)

That belongs to Tyler. (Lacks clarity)

That **day planner** belongs to Tyler. (Provides clarity)

These are from Jacob. (Lacks clarity)

These **recommendations** are from Jacob. (Provides clarity)

Those are mine. (Lacks clarity)

Those **books** are mine. (Provides clarity)

5. Eliminate expletives. An expletive is a meaningless word—a word that adds nothing to the sentence or a word that does not provide clarity in the sentence. Some examples of expletives that you should use with caution in writing are *it is, it was, there is,* and *there are.*

There are many implications to his behavior. (Emphasizes an expletive)

Many implications **are evident** in his behavior. (Emphasizes the important words in the sentence)

It is *your reputation that is at stake.* (Emphasizes an expletive)

Your reputation **is** at stake. (Emphasizes the important words in the sentence)

Writing Sentences

1. Avoid beginning a sentence with an expletive.

There are three people absent from the office today. (Emphasizes *there*)

Three people **are** absent from the office today. (Emphasizes *three people*)

2. Write "positive" sentences rather than "negative" sentences—tell what *can* be done instead of what *cannot* be done.

GEI will *not* call you until July 15. (Negative)

GEI *will* call you on July 15. (Positive)

3. Use an "active" voice to present "positive" ideas. (The subject does the acting)

Steve *wrote* the report. (Active voice)

Wendy *completed* the job in three days. (Active voice)

4. Use a "passive" voice to present "negative" ideas. (The subject is acted upon)

The report *was delayed* by Steve. (Passive voice)

The job *was completed* by Wendy after the due date. (Passive voice)

5. Place an idea in a "simple sentence" to emphasize that idea.

Scott was absent from the office today. (Simple sentence)

Amy missed one day of work last week. (Simple sentence)

6. Place an idea in a "compound sentence" to de-emphasize that idea.

Scott was absent from the office today, but he was here yesterday.

Amy missed one day of work last week, but she was ill.

7. Place an idea in an "independent clause" for de-emphasis.

Although Julie was absent from work today, she was here yesterday. (Dependent clause; independent clause)

Even though James missed work last week, he managed to complete the report. (Dependent clause; independent clause)

8. Use a word more than once in a sentence to emphasize that word.

The day was a *success,* and that *success* was due to your willingness to serve as hostess.

The *thought* was meaningless, but that *thought* was accepted by most of the people.

Writing Paragraphs

1. Avoid changes in thought that are too abrupt. Link each sentence to a preceding sentence.

The workers enjoyed the pay increase. The pay increase was long overdue.

Audrey retired from GEI last June. Her retirement was not anticipated.

2. Use small words and short sentences to make an exciting paragraph.

We will *endeavor* to be there on time. We *contemplate* whether or not all employees should attend.

We will *try* to be there on time. Should all employees attend?

3. Strive for short paragraphs. Vary the length of the paragraphs.

4. Strive for paragraphs that are consistently *deductive* or consistently *inductive.*

Inductive: details appear first followed by the main idea.

Deductive: main idea appears first followed by details.

5. Create emphasis in paragraphs by placing an important sentence either first (rule of primacy) or by placing the important sentence last (rule of recency).

Punctuation and Capitalization

Commas

- Use a comma after parts of a date.

She came to work for us March 31, 2000, at our Cleveland branch.

On Thursday, March 3, 2000, I left the firm.

- Use a comma after parts of an address.

Tina lives at 2987 East Punxsutawney Street, Girard, OH 48987.

Lourdes moved to 435 Northeast Blinton Road, Bergholz, OH 43908. (No comma between state and ZIP)

- Use a comma to separate items in a series. Use a comma *before* the last item.

  Bill likes apples, oranges, peaches, and pears.

  They played at our house, in the park, and at the zoo.

- Use a comma after *yes, no, oh,* and *well* when these words are used at the beginning of a sentence.

  Yes, I'll be in class tomorrow.

  No, Alfredo will not attend the commencement.

  Well, I think you've said enough.

  Oh, I don't think so.

- Use a comma after directly addressing someone.

  Deidre, have you seen my wallet?

  No, Tom, I haven't seen your wallet.

  Little girl, are you performing in the dance recital this evening?

- Use a comma to separate *too* (when it means *also*) from the remainder of the sentence.

  Did you attend the conference, too?

  Thursday, too, was a hectic day.

- Use a comma to set off parenthetical expressions (words or phrases not necessary to the meaning of the sentence).

  College football, for example, is truly exciting.

  Therefore, Letitia gave me all of the money.

  Sky diving, however, is an extremely dangerous sport.

- Use a comma to set off an appositive (words or phrases that explain the word they follow).

  Bill is a friend of Mr. Schneider, the marketing professor.

  That antique, which I purchased yesterday, is priceless.

- Use commas to set off *nonrestrictive* clauses (word or words not necessary to the meaning of the sentence.)

  My automobile, which does not have a full-size spare tire, is out of gas.

  That antique, which I purchased yesterday, is priceless.

Periods

- Use a period after a declarative or imperative sentence (a sentence that states a fact or a command).

  The teacher quit her job yesterday. (Declarative)

  Give me that knife immediately. (Imperative)

- Use a period with abbreviations.

  Jack Smithers, Jr.

  Ms. Mary Lou Gonzalez

  2:00 p.m.

  Dr. Russell Turkistan

  (*Note:* Two-letter state abbreviations do *not* require periods.)

- Use a period with initials.

  Send the package C.O.D.

  Marilda Collins is chair of the P.T.A. this year.

  Wake me at two p.m.

Semicolons

- Use semicolons between items in a series if the items contain commas.

  Those relatives in attendance were from Chicago, Illinois; Denver, Colorado; Los Angeles, California; and Keller, Texas.

  The new officers are Tom Lauterbur, president; Juanita Portales, secretary; and Ma Wan Lei, treasurer.

- Use a semicolon between two complete sentences when *not* joined by a coordinate conjunction such as *and, but, or, for, yet.*

  Brunhilda's team won the game; the team plays again tomorrow.

  The minister delivered the sermon; no one listened.

- Use a semicolon before a *conjunctive adverb* that connects two complete sentences.

  Punctuation and grammar are a lot of fun; however, one must study every day.

  Her work will be completed on time; therefore, you must submit the material now.

Colons

- Use a colon to show that something is to follow.

  Please bring the following materials to work: a hammer, several nails, a screwdriver, and a wrench. (The part of the sentence *before* the colon must sound as though it is a complete sentence.)

- Use a colon after the salutation of a business letter.

  Dear Mr. Lundquist:

  Dear Professor Habib:

- Use a colon when using numbers to indicate time, volume, or page.

  Send the receipt by 3:30 p.m.

  You'll find that citation in Smith's article, 7:37 (meaning volume 7, page 37).

Quotation Marks

- Use quotation marks to enclose a direct clause.

  "I'll never do that again," she promised.

  "Give me musicians who will play their best," Rolf remarked, "and I'll show you the best orchestra in the world."

- Use quotation marks with words used in a special sense, such as *ironical, coined,* or *technical.*

  Marcella was considered an "expert" in making apple pie.

  Helene's car "died" on the freeway.

- Use a *single quotation mark* to enclose a quotation within a quotation.

  She told me "Adam said this to Eve, 'try the big red apple at the top of the tree.'"

- Place closing quotation marks *outside* a period or comma.

  That car is a "lemon."

  That car is a "lemon," she thought.

- Place quotation marks *outside* if a question mark or exclamation point is part of the quotation.

She said, "Get out of here!"

She yelled, "What kind of fool am I?"

- Place question marks and exclamation points that are *not* part of the quotation *outside* of the quotation marks.

    She said, "The quarterback got thrown out of the game"!

    Did she say, "The quarterback got thrown out of the game"?

Apostrophes

- Use an apostrophe then an *s* to show singular possession.

    Matilda's car is in the garage.

    Somebody borrowed Tim's baseball glove.

- Use an *s* then an apostrophe to show *plural* possession.

    Somebody borrowed all of the boys' baseball gloves.

    The factories' products are sold all over the world.

- Use an apostrophe and *s* in the last word of a compound adjective before a noun.

    My mother-in-law's only purpose in life is to have fun.

    The thief stole my sister-in-law's boat last night.

Hyphens

- Use a hyphen to divide words between syllables at the end of a line.

    He likes to have con-
      versation with anybody he meets.

    Joseph Lucci was *stopped* by the traffic officer. (Stopped is only one syllable; not divided)

- Use a hyphen with a compound adjective when it *precedes* the word being modified.

    Alberto Mendez is a well-known person in social circles.

    We moved to the fourth-floor office early last year.

    But

    Alberto Mendez is a person well known in social circles. (no hyphen)

    We moved to the office on the fourth floor early last year. (no hyphen)

- Use a hyphen in compound numbers and with fractions.

    Grandma Mackenzie turned seventy-seven last month.

    Forty-three people attended the class reunion.

    Please pour me one-third glass of milk.

- Use a hyphen when the word is confusing.

    Will you please *reform* the model on which you are working.

    Will you please *re-form* the model on which you are working.

- Use a hyphen with compound titles.

    Constantine Demetrious is the new president-elect of the honor society.

    Greg Paxton is an ex-student of mine.

Dashes and Parentheses

- Use a dash to indicate an abrupt change of thought or to indicate a parenthetical expression.

My ex-wife—bless her soul—just got married to my ex-best friend.

His latest novel—have you read it?—is exciting as well as interesting.

(*Note:* The dash is approximately twice the size of the *hyphen.*)

- Use parentheses to indicate numbered sections within sentences.

Please give me (1) red apples, (2) green grapes, and (3) yellow lemons.

- Use parentheses to enclose words that explain.

Monica Lewis (the girls' basketball coach) resigned yesterday.

Capitalization

- Use a capital letter for the first word in a sentence.

The first word in a sentence requires capitalization.

Thirty people attended the party. (Spell out a number when it begins a sentence.)

- Use capital letters to indicate the first word in a direct quotation.

The preacher said to us, "I hope you will all be here next Sunday."

Monica reported, "There is no school tomorrow."

- Use capital letters for names, initials, and titles of persons.

Roger Lodger is a draft dodger.

Professor Mills is away from campus for a month.

Ricardo Juarez, Ph.D., is my brother-in-law.

- Use capital letters for days of the week and months of the year.

Tuesday is my birthday.

Saturday, August 1, is the anniversary of my parents.

(Note: Do *not* capitalize the seasons: spring, summer, fall, winter.)

- Use capital letters for nationalities, races, languages, and religions.

Guenther is German.

Indira is an Indian from New Delhi.

He enrolled in a course in Spanish, but he failed it.

Mike is Jewish; Megan is Catholic; and Henry is Protestant.

- Use capital letters for geographical names.

The Pacific Ocean is colder and deeper than the Atlantic Ocean.

Her favorite city in all the world is Athens.

We will visit Yosemite Park in California this summer.

- Use capital letters for names of organizations.

Johnny is an Eagle Scout with the Boy Scouts of America.

The Cleveland Orchestra is one of the world's finest symphony orchestras.

- Use capital letters for names of books, magazines, newspapers, works of art, and musical compositions.

Have you read *Tuesdays with Morrie*? (Place book names in italics.)

No, but I do read the *Cleveland Plain Dealer* on a daily basis.

Last summer I visited the Prado Museum in Madrid and saw a reproduction of Michelangelo's David.